	BEATVS	PETRVS
	NATIONE	ANTIBIOCENVS
II	Linus	Nat · Itals
III	Eletus ·	Nat · Romans ·
IIII	Clemens ·	Nat · grecis
V	Anacletus	Nat · grecis
VI	Cuuaristus	Nat · grecis
VII	Alexander	Nat · rom
VIII	Xristus I	Nat · rom
VIIII	Thelesphor ·	Nat · grecis
X	Yginus	Nat · grecis
XI	Pius ·	Nat · Itals
XII	Anecitus ·	Nat · Sirus
XIII	Sother	Nat · Campans
XIIII	Eleuther ·	Nat · grecis
XV	Victor	Nat · Afer
XVI	Zephorinus ·	Nat · rom ·
XVII	Calistus ·	Nat · rom ·
XVIII	Urbanus ·	Nat · rom ·
XVIIII	Pontianus ·	Nat · rom ·
XX	Antheros ·	Nat · grec ·
XXI	Fabianus ·	Nat · rom ·
XXII	Cornelius ·	Nat · rom ·
XXIII	Lucius ·	Nat · rom ·
XXIIII	Stephanus · I	Nat · rom
XXV	Sixtus II	Nat · grecis
XXVI	Dionisius ·	Nat · N. possum inueni re it.

THE MEDIEVAL PAPACY

GEOFFREY BARRACLOUGH

HARCOURT, BRACE & WORLD, INC.

Frontispiece

1 A list of the first twenty-six 'popes' (or bishops of Rome), starting with St Peter and going down to Dionysius (259–68). These lists exist in a number of different versions. The present one, copied at St Amand *c*. 800, shows St Clement, traditionally St Peter's successor and first bishop of Rome, in the third place, after Linus and Cletus (or Anencletus)

First American Edition 1968

Reprinted 1970

Library of Congress Catalog Card Number: 68-29667

PRINTED IN GREAT BRITAIN BY JARROLD AND SONS LTD, NORWICH

CONTENTS

There was a time, not so long ago, when it would have been as bold, and foolhardy, to write a history of the Medieval Papacy as to put one's foot in a hornet's nest. Circumstances today are happily different. Co-existence, reunion and sweetness are the current watchwords, and even the two age-old antagonists, Rome and Constantinople, whose passionate doctrinal disputes reach back so much further than those of Catholics and Protestants, are ready to kiss each other on both cheeks and make friends.

But if the old controversies have abated, they have left echoes behind and have been succeeded by new disputes, more sophisticated, perhaps, but no less bitter, and pursued with that peculiar self-righteousness and vindictiveness of which only scholars are capable. It would be foolish to suppose that I can escape the backlash. In fact, I have drawn gratefully on the work of Catholic and Protestant writers, and of those who are professedly neither, and I am unaware that I have any confessional axe to grind; but I cannot deny, or hope to extricate myself entirely from, my Protestant background and upbringing.

It should hardly be necessary to add that the approach adopted in this volume is historical; that is to say, I have treated the papacy as an historical phenomenon, developing and changing in response to changing historical circumstances. By this I do not mean to imply that the historian can ignore the central doctrines of the medieval papacy – the dogmas of 'Petrine succession' and papal 'primacy', for example, or the concept of 'plenitude of power' – but rather that he will view them in their historical context, as historically conditioned claims, and not, as a student of dogmatic theology might do, as unchanging principles.

'Theorists', a Catholic historian in England recently wrote, 'seem to credit words with the power of sticks and stones to break bones.' That is not the view I have adopted in this volume. I have been concerned not so much with the great controversies between church and state, or papacy and empire, which historians are so apt to stress, as with the position of the papacy in the church, using the word 'church' both in the wider sense of the whole community of the faithful, and in the narrower sense of the ecclesiastical hierarchy, of which the bishop of Rome was a part. I have tried to show the polarity between the papacy's political preoccupations and its pastoral duties, and how the resultant tensions affected both the church and the

papacy itself. Mindful of Paul Sabatier's famous distinction between 'religion of the law' and 'religion of the spirit', I have sought to indicate the
way the very success of the papacy in building up its authority and its legal
and administrative machinery militated against its claim to spiritual leadership, and how an institution which rose through furthering the cause of
reform later became an obstacle to reform and itself in need of reformation.
I have been concerned, in other words, with the great dichotomies which
run through the history of the medieval papacy. It may be that this approach
lacks the grand sweep and logical coherence which a more theoretical treatment might convey; but it may be some compensation if it enables the
reader to understand better the tensions and complexities – to say nothing
of the conflicting ideals and contrasting personalities – which make the history of the medieval papacy so dramatic and at the same time so instructive
a story.

It is now almost forty years ago since, under the direction of a great
Catholic historian, Rudolf von Heckel, I began to study the history of the
medieval papacy. In the course of my work, at Rome and elsewhere, I was
fortunate in having before my eyes his example of dedicated scholarship,
and that of other distinguished scholars, Catholic and Protestant, whom I
was privileged to know. They include – to mention only a few of those no
longer with us – Cardinal Franz Ehrle and Cardinal Angelo Mercati, whose
help and encouragement were so readily given; Paul Kehr, and the distinguished band of scholars gathered round him in Rome, whose great
work in collecting together the documentary records of the early medieval
papacy revealed so many new aspects of its history; Ulrich Stutz, who completely transformed our conception of the early medieval church; Johannes
Haller, whose brilliant critical mind dispelled so many shadows and de-
lighted even those who rarely agreed with his conclusions; Ferdinand Lot,
no specialist on the papacy, but a masterly historian of the environment in
which it grew; and, last but not least, George Gordon Coulton, last survivor
of the old school of Protestant controversialists, whose vast knowledge and
sympathetic understanding of medieval Christianity have never received
their due. What I learnt, from them and others, is that the most significant
differences of interpretation cut across the conventional lines of demarca-
tion, and that the important criterion for the historian is not whether a
writer is Catholic or Protestant, but how scrupulously he handles historical
evidence. By this criterion some of the most learned and ambitious writing
will be found wanting.

G. BARRACLOUGH

8

St John's College, Cambridge
September 1967

It is one of the great paradoxes of history that the papacy, as we think of it today, is in most essential ways a creation of medieval Europe. According to the dogma of the Catholic church, as defined at the First Vatican Council in 1870, the papacy owed its institution to St Peter, and the Roman pontiff, as St Peter's successor, inherited the supreme authority bestowed by Christ upon the 'prince of the apostles'. Nevertheless the exercise of this authority, as one of the greatest Catholic canon lawyers of the nineteenth century pointed out, was always subject to circumstances of time and place. Even the concept of papal primacy was only established by slow and painful stages, and many centuries were to pass after its theoretical formulation in the days of pope Leo I (440–61) before theory was translated into practice. The establishment of an effective papal monarchy, exercising a 'plenitude of power' over the whole Catholic church, was still far from completion when the twelfth century began.

When we say that the papacy was a creation of medieval Europe, what we mean, therefore, is that it was during the middle ages that the Roman church developed from obscure beginnings as a small persecuted community in the capital of the Roman empire, into a world-embracing institution endowed, as the First Vatican Council affirmed, with 'the supreme power of governing the universal church'. It was not until the sixth century, and then only in the west, that the title 'papa' – originally used to express the fatherly care bestowed by any and every bishop on his flock – began to be reserved for the bishop of Rome. Even as late as 1075 it was still necessary for Gregory VII to insist that there was only one pope in the world. There is a great temptation for the historian to regard the history of the papacy as a logical process, dominated by the unswerving application of a few fundamental principles, and to admire the tenacity of purpose through which, step by step, the popes realized a pre-existing 'doctrinal programme.' In reality, this picture of 'steady continuity,' though it dominated both Catholic and Protestant writing for many generations, reflects a one-sided, aprioristic approach to the historical facts. Many of the developments which contributed to the rise of the papacy were accidental and unforeseen, and quite outside the pope's control; and papal decisions which in retrospect seem to form part of a coherent plan, were in reality piecemeal reactions to particular circumstances and situations. It was only in the eleventh century that a generation inspired by hierocratic ideals saw them as links in a chain reaching back in unbroken continuity to St Peter.

If it would be unhistorical and misleading to suggest that successive popes pursued one consistent policy, directed to a single clearly conceived end, it is also true that this fact does not detract from the significance of the story. For six centuries or more the papacy was a major force shaping the destinies of Europe. The success of the Roman church in weathering the storms of centuries may seem, to some, so remarkable that it can only be rationally explained as the result of the working of divine providence; while others will admire at least its ability to adapt itself – as it is still doing today – to the circumstances of a changing world.

Few institutions in the whole of history have shown an equal capacity for survival. Its history is the story of the way it came to terms with the different environments in which it was placed: the Roman empire, the Germanic kingdoms of the early middle ages, the national states which were visibly rising in the fifteenth century, and today the 'third world' of Asia and Africa. It is characteristic of the church, whose ultimate end is not in this world, that it has never irrevocably identified itself with any existing social or political system. From most it has taken, and to all it has given; and in the process it has transformed itself and its position in the world. It is this process that we shall follow in the succeeding pages of this book beginning with the impact on the Roman church of the Roman empire, which contributed so much to its organization, and of the Germanic peoples, particularly the Anglo-Saxons, who contributed so much to its moral standing.

The bishop of Rome, at the time of Constantine the Great, was in no sense a pope and laid no claim to the position of pope. The very idea of the papacy had still to be formulated, and if we use the word to describe the position of the bishop of Rome at this early period, we must never forget that we are referring to something very different in essence from the papacy of later times. It is true, of course, that the early centuries, which saw the gradual rise of the bishop of Rome to a position of primacy, prepared the way for the emergence of the papacy; and for that reason they have an integral place in the story. They were nevertheless only a period of preparation; and for that reason we shall pass over them shortly, without entering into all the controversies to which they have given rise. It was when the bishop of Rome became more than a bishop of Rome, and more than the

VICARIVSVRBISROMAE

2 Representation
of 'the vicar
of the city
of Rome',
c. 400

first bishop of the Roman empire, that the history of the papacy began;
and this was only after the dark days of the seventh century, when (as
Ferdinand Lot once wrote) it seemed as though Mediterranean civilization
was on the point of collapse and would drag the church down with it into
bankruptcy. It was not until this crisis had been surmounted that the papacy
emerged as one of the great formative influences in European history.

3 St Peter and St Paul, the apostles who were referred to in early tradition as joint founders of the Roman church. From a gold glass, probably fourth century

The historian who, through the mists of time, tries to trace his way back to the origins of the Roman church, finds very little fact and a great deal of conjecture. He is confronted by a massive accretion of later tradition and myth, but an almost total lack of contemporary record. This is not surprising. So long as Christianity remained a messianic creed, living in the daily expectation of the end of the world and the second coming, purely historical phenomena had little relevance. There is good evidence that there were Christians among the Jewish community in Rome by AD 49; it is certain that St Paul visited them and preached to them around AD 61–3, and probable – though direct evidence is lacking – that he was executed there in AD 67. Most scholars, Protestant and Catholic alike, believe that St Peter also preached in Rome and met his death at about the same time; but this view is based entirely on later tradition, first clearly articulated about AD 170 by Irenæus and Dionysius of Corinth. It is also probable that the early Christian community, still treated by Romans as a Jewish sect, was virtually eliminated in the persecution of the Jews which followed the burning of Rome in AD 64. When it was rebuilt, and how, we do not know; but it is hardly too much to suppose that a tribulation of this magnitude resulted in a shattering breach of continuity and tradition.

In all this there is no indication that the early Christian community in Rome was presided over by a bishop. This again is not surprising. The early Christian churches were small communities, bound together by faith and brotherly love, which had no need for a monarchical head. Within each congregation, no doubt, a few men – distinguished preachers or early converts – stood out as 'elders' and 'overseers'. As 'shepherds' of their flock, they were called indifferently 'bishops' (ἐπίσκοποι) and 'presbyters' (πρεσβύτεροι); and for the dispensing of alms and other tasks the communities soon appointed deacons and deaconesses. But such authority as they possessed they exercised in common, and it was only in the second half of the second century that the grades in the hierarchy were defined and differentiated and the 'bishop' drew ahead as the appointed leader of his church. In this development Rome was not noticeably prominent. Rather it began in the east, and can only be traced in Rome from the time of

Hippolytus in the early third century. Nevertheless it is significant that the first lists of the bishops of Rome date from AD 160–85; that they make Peter and Paul conjointly the founders of the Roman church; and that none asserts that St Peter himself was bishop. Only about AD 220, in the time of pope Callistus, does the practice arise of reckoning Peter as the first bishop of Rome; and it was another twenty or thirty years before the tradition took shape according to which, shortly before his death, St Peter 'laid hands' upon Clement – who, in the earlier lists, appears in the third place, after Linus and Anencletus – as 'bishop of the Romans' and entrusted him with his 'chair of discourse'.

There were weighty reasons why, in Rome as elsewhere, the office of bishop should develop as Christianity took root, and why so much emphasis was laid upon the maintenance of a tradition reaching back in unbroken succession to the apostles. The very weakness of organization which marked the early church, its lack of a recognized canon of scriptures, and the scope it left for charismatic leaders, wandering preachers, zealots and mystics, threatened its existence. Already early in the second century it seemed to be breaking apart into small unstable sects, often at odds with one another, and apparently doomed quickly to perish altogether. The development of the episcopacy was an answer to this threat, and to the more serious challenges thrown out towards the end of the century by Montanists, Gnostics, Adoptionists, the followers of Marcion and other similar movements. The bishop became the custodian of orthodoxy – 'ubi episcopus, ibi ecclesia' – and from the middle of the third century bishops from neighbouring cities began to meet together in synods to define doctrine and combat heresy. In this way, ecclesiastical provinces under metropolitans came into existence, mostly modelled on the existing imperial provincial organization.

But more than closer organization was needed, if the church was to maintain its position against the schismatics, and it was Irenæus, who became bishop of Lyons in AD 178, who pointed the way forward. How could it be shown that sectaries, such as the Montanists, were wrong in their interpretation of Christian tradition and belief? The answer was provided by Irenæus, and after him by Tertullian of Carthage, writing about AD 198, who developed the theory of apostolic succession. Those churches, and those churches alone, which could trace their descent from one of the apostles, were repositories of the true faith, which the apostles had handed down. What Christ revealed to them, Tertullian wrote,

can only be proved by the same churches which those apostles founded....

Was anything hidden from Peter, who was called the rock on which the Church would be built, who received the keys of the Kingdom of Heaven, and the power of loosing and binding in heaven and on earth? Was anything hidden from John, the most beloved of the Lord, who leaned upon his breast, and to whom alone the Lord foretold the treachery of Judas?

It is against this background that the rise of the bishop of Rome must be set. The idea of apostolic succession was, of course, in no way identified with Rome. There were many other churches – Jerusalem, Antioch, Ephesus, Smyrna, Philippi, Thessalonica, Corinth – which claimed descent from one or other of the apostles; and Alexandria was not slow to join their ranks by appropriating Mark as its founder. Irenæus and Tertullian were not arguing on behalf of Rome; their concern was to assert episcopal authority as such, not papal authority or the authority of the Roman bishop. Antioch and Corinth, as well as Rome, claimed descent from St Peter. But Rome was the only apostolic church in the western half of the Roman empire, and, perhaps because they both came from the west, there is no doubt that Irenæus and Tertullian both placed special emphasis on Rome. Irenæus, in a famous but ambiguous and hotly disputed passage, wrote of the 'more powerful principality' of the Roman church, on account of which all other churches should live in harmony with it. Tertullian laid weight on the special authority of Rome, which alone incorporated the tradition of three apostles – Peter, Paul and John – but at the same time emphasized the special position of Peter. It was, in fact, Tertullian, the outstanding theologian of the Latin west before Augustine, who took in hand the speculative interpretation of the famous New Testament texts – *Tu es Petrus*, and the like – which established the unique prerogatives of Peter as the first of the apostles, and therewith of the Roman church as Peter's special foundation.

Before that point was reached there was nevertheless far to go. Tertullian himself regarded the powers conferred by Christ on Peter, so far as they were not entirely personal, as the attribute of the whole Christian church, not of the bishop of Rome alone. But the emphasis on Peter persisted; and the see of Rome, where the apostle was believed to be buried, could not but profit. It is hardly accidental that evidence – confirmed by recent excavations – for the veneration of the shrine of St Peter at the Vatican dates from the last quarter of the second century. Whether his grave, or that of Paul on the Ostian Way, was or was not genuine, there is no doubt that the

4 A second-century tomb discovered in recent excavations below St Peter's in Rome; it was here, according to ancient tradition, that St Peter was buried

close bodily association with Peter was an advantage the bishop of Rome could exploit, if occasion arose. And precisely this was what occurred in the course of the third century when questions such as the celebration of Easter or the remission of sins led to fierce doctrinal controversies. The arguments Irenæus and Tertullian had developed against the sectaries were now turned against other churches. Thus Victor I (189–98) broke off relations with the churches of Asia Minor, because they would not accept his ruling in the Easter dispute, and Callistus I (217–22), for the first time directly invoking Petrine authority, sought in the most peremptory manner to impose his doctrine of penance on all other churches.

Neither was successful; but it is difficult not to see in their actions a deliberate attempt to assert the authority, if not the primacy, of Rome. The next stage came a generation later, with Stephen I (254–57), who, if his opponents are to be believed, specifically claimed a 'primacy', boasting (as Firmilian, bishop of Caesarea, wrote) 'about the place of his bishopric' and insisting 'that he holds his succession from Peter.' It was Stephen who adopted the phrase *cathedra Petri* (or 'chair of Peter'), which had been coined by his contemporary and opponent, St Cyprian of Carthage, and, contrary to Cyprian's own intention, made it a basis from which, later, the primatial rights of the Roman church were developed.

16

After Stephen there was little progress in the theoretical formulation of papal rights until popes Damasus (366–84) and Leo I (440–61). In practice, Stephen's pronouncements had no visible effect. The church, in organization, was still a federation of episcopal churches, each with its own customs and usages, loosely ruled by synods, and only by straining the evidence can it be argued that any special authority was vested in the bishop of Rome. Cyprian's conception of the church as resting on the unity of the bishops and their co-operation still prevailed. Moreover, the renewal of persecution under the emperor Decius (249–51), which continued with intermissions down to 311, struck the church of Rome with particular severity. In August 258 pope Xystus and the whole of the diaconal college were executed, and many months passed before the church of the capital nerved itself to elect a new bishop; and when the persecution was renewed under Aurelian and Diocletian – 'the most systematic attempt to destroy Christianity which the Roman state ever assayed' – thousands of Christians, including apparently pope Marcellinus himself, fell away into apostasy. In these circumstances the Roman church had enough to do to keep its head above water. This was no time for doctrinal controversies or the airing of theoretical claims to a position of special authority, but rather for unity in the face of the external threat.

5, 6 Two bishops of Rome in the period of persecution, Xystus II (257–8), martyred under the emperor Valentinian, and Marcellinus (296–304), who is alleged to have apostatized during the persecutions of Diocletian

In fact, however, the church of Rome owed its eminence not so much to theoretical claims, which few were willing to concede, as to its position in the Roman empire. The obvious centre of the Christian faith in the early days was Jerusalem, where James, the brother of Christ, was active; but James's martyrdom in AD 62 and the destruction of Jerusalem in AD 70 opened the way for Rome. Until AD 286, when Diocletian moved the seats of government to Nicomedia and Milan, the church of Rome was the church of the metropolis, and the advantages this fact conferred were immense. Rome, as capital of the empire, was a natural focus to which (as Irenæus wrote) 'on account of its commanding position . . . the faithful from everywhere must needs resort'. Contacts with the imperial government were easy, and this was important, particularly under the dynasty of Severus (193–235), which was favourably disposed to Christianity. It meant that the church of Rome could intervene with the authorities on behalf of other churches; it meant also that it soon accumulated wealth with which to help less fortunate congregations. Dionysius of Corinth, writing about AD 170, states that it was 'the custom of the Romans . . . from the beginning . . . to assist all the brotherhood in various ways and send contributions to churches in every city, thus relieving the want of the needy.'

The esteem which the Roman church acquired in this way needs no emphasis; and its advantages as the church of the imperial capital and its ecclesiastical prestige, as the church of 'the two most glorious apostles, Peter and Paul', reinforced each other. It is impossible to say with finality which came first, or which contributed more to its rise to pre-eminence. Even if the martyrdom of the apostles in Rome was a legend, it was an effective one; and the number of martyrs Rome suffered both in the early persecutions under Nero, and in later persecutions under Decius and Valerian, added immeasurably to its religious prestige.

It goes without saying that this prestige, and the authority it conferred, belonged originally to the Roman church, or to the Christian community in Rome as a whole, and not to the Roman bishop. It goes without saying also that, as the position of the Roman bishop was consolidated, he began to assume the authority which came to him as head of the Roman church. Until late in the second century the bishop of Rome was the only bishop in Italy; and the fact that Rome was the only apostolic church in the whole of the west placed him at least on a level of parity with the bishops of the great eastern sees, such as Antioch and Alexandria. These facts paved the way for the developments of the fourth and fifth centuries; but in AD 313, when persecution had ceased and Christianity was on the way to becoming the official religion of the Roman empire, 'the power of the Roman pontiff, and his relation to the universal church, were' (in the words of a great Catholic historian) 'not yet fully developed'. A few tentative claims had been made, a position of considerable influence and prestige had been built up; but the bishop of Rome was still only a bishop among bishops and the characteristic doctrines of papal primacy had still to be systematically formulated.

The reconciliation between Constantine the Great and the Christian church, marked by the handing over in 312 of the Lateran palace to bishop Miltiades as an episcopal residence, profoundly affected the position of the papacy. To begin with, it is true, Christianity was only tolerated, and it was not until 391 that Theodosius I finally prohibited heathen cults and made the Christian faith the official religion of the Roman state. But already under Constantine it enjoyed the status of 'most favoured religion', and privileges and benefactions showered on the Roman church. Constantine himself ordered the erection of a large and imposing basilica over St Peter's shrine in the Vatican; his mother, Helena, built another, the church known today

7 Emperor Theodosius the Great, during whose reign Christianity was proclaimed the official state religion of the Roman empire

as Santa Croce in Gerusalemme, near the Lateran. Miltiades himself, or his successor, Sylvester I (314–35), began in 314 the construction of the great Lateran basilica adjacent to the new papal palace, which from that time forward down to the present day has remained the official seat of the bishop of Rome. A little after the middle of the fourth century Optatus of Mileve wrote with pride of the forty basilicas which adorned the city; and the Christian poet Prudentius, writing about 400, draws an impressive picture of the new grandeur, 'the Tiber . . . flowing between the consecrated sepulchres', the colonnaded courts, rich tombs and ceremonious rituals.

Other benefactions, less spectacular but no less substantial, quickly accrued. Constantine himself made grants from the state treasury, and the church began to accumulate estates and rely more and more on revenue from properties and endowments bestowed by emperors, officials and wealthy individuals, instead of depending for its income on the small, voluntary donations contributed week by week by the rank and file of ordinary Christians. But if, in material ways, the church profited from its association with the state, in other respects the new relationship created new problems; and it is the latter which primarily concern us here, since, from the point of view of the bishop of Rome, it was the problem of adjustment to the changed situation which led to most of the important developments, down at least to the death of pope Gregory I in 604.

8 A sixteenth-century engraving of the church of Santa Croce in Gerusalemme, founded by Helen, mother of Constantine the Great

9 The Lateran palace and basilica in Rome, the pope's titular church and seat of papal government throughout the Middle Ages; a sixteenth-century engraving

There is no doubt, in the first place, that the sudden change in the attitude of the imperial government, from persecution to toleration and support, found the church largely unprepared. From Sixtus II (257–58) to Damasus I (366–84), the popes were mediocre, if not entirely shadowy figures, who simply reacted to events without showing any real capacity to shape the new relationship. The first churchman to face the issues squarely, and attempt a definition of the relations of church and state was, characteristically, not the pope but St Ambrose of Milan (*c.* 340–97). Constantine, on the other hand, has been described – perhaps too harshly – as at once a 'benefactor, tyrant and evil genius'. Certainly his attitude towards Christianity was not disinterested. He saw it as an instrument of cohesion, a pillar of the new imperial structure he was building, a 'state religion' to underpin his government; and as such he had no intention of leaving it alone. In particular, the diversity of belief and practice, which had been so characteristic of the church as long as it was a loose federation, was no longer tolerable.

This was seen immediately when, after inconclusive synods at Rome, Carthage and Arles, the emperor personally passed sentence on the Donatists in 316. It was made even plainer in 325, at the famous council of Nicaea, when Constantine sought to settle the Arian controversy by imposing his own formula. He regarded the empire, as he told pope Miltiades, as entrusted to him by divine providence, and his 'reverence for the legitimate Catholic church' was such that he did 'not wish to leave schism or division in any place.' This meant, in effect, that he had no hesitation about interfering, where necessary, in the internal affairs of the church; precisely because God's favour to the empire depended on 'the honesty of the priesthood', the state of the church (as Justinian was later to write) was necessarily a main concern of the emperors.

The first obstacle to the rise of papal power, under the new dispensation, was therefore the attitude of the imperial government to the church, which persisted even after the emperor abandoned the heathen title, *pontifex maximus*, in 379. This is not the place to describe the imperial theocracy, which reached its peak under Justinian (527–65). Justinian's brutal measures – the violent deposition of Silverius (536–37), who died in a penal colony, the harrying and imprisonment of Vigilius (537–55), and the enforced appointment of the unworthy Pelagius I (556–61) – are notorious, but they were by no means typical. Although the emperor's powers were frequently abused, it would be a mistake to regard the system as specifically directed against the papacy. Harassed by the great Christological controversies of the fourth and fifth centuries, which were rending the empire, the emperors were ready to resort to any authority which might serve as a unifying force, and among these the church of Rome, with the prestige it derived from St Peter, was eminent. It is therefore not surprising to find the emperor Gratian, in 378, supporting the Roman bishop's claim to authority over the other bishops of the west, or Theodosius I and his two co-emperors recognizing, in 380, the bishop of Rome as the guardian of the true faith and specifically reserving for those who espoused his doctrines the title of 'Catholic Christians'. And in 445 Valentinian III, going far beyond the precedent set by Gratian, laid down that 'whatsoever the authority of the apostolic see has sanctioned, or shall sanction, shall be the law for all.'

It is not difficult, taking these various pronouncements and arranging them in chronological order, to see a gradual recognition and consolidation of papal authority over the church. In actual fact the position was a good deal more complicated. In the first place, there is the question whether they applied to the Christian church as a whole, or only to the western provinces.

But more important is the fact that, so far as the emperors were concerned, they were only tactical manœuvres. What they were concerned with, above all else, was unity of faith; and it was because 'ancient usage' – as Valentinian III said – gave the Roman bishop 'a pre-eminence above all others in the episcopate to judge in matters of faith', that they supported him. If Rome failed them, they had other instruments to hand. One was the general synod, or general council, which, beginning with the council of Nicaea in 325, Constantine the Great evidently envisaged as the supreme tribunal of the church; and it is significant that Valentinian III, whose support of papal authority in 445 has just been noted, had earlier expressed his wish for 'sacred doctrine to be discussed and examined in a holy synod'. 'They ought to be judges', he wrote, 'who preside over the priesthood everywhere.' The other instrument of the emperors was the bishopric of Constantinople which, after Constantine had definitely moved the seat of government to the east, could claim, as Rome had done before, to be the metropolitan church of the empire, was better acquainted than Rome with the ecclesiastical and theological problems of the eastern provinces, and, nearer at hand, was more easily subjected to imperial influence.

These were the competing powers with which, as a result of Christianity becoming a 'state religion', the papacy had to contend. They were not the only ones. Just as Constantine's transference of the capital to the east brought it face to face with Constantinople, so the division of the empire in 395 and the transfer of the government of the western half first to Milan in 286 and then to Ravenna in 402, raised up competing powers nearer home. The remarkable rise of the church of Milan, as a result of its connection with the official residence of the western emperor, indicates clearly how much Rome, in an earlier age, had owed to its position as the church of the capital. Now Rome was sinking to the level of a provincial city, and the Roman church, forced to surrender jurisdiction over the whole of northern Italy to Milan, was sinking with it. It was against these pressures that the popes of the fifth and sixth centuries reacted, by defining and asserting their prerogatives and building up the doctrine of papal primacy.

The reaction began under Damasus I (366–84) and continued until the end of the pontificate of Gregory I (590–604), and it would be hard, on any impartial review of the evidence, to deny that the main incentive driving the bishop of old Rome to formulate his rights was the threat to his position implicit in the ambitions of the bishop of 'new Rome'. These ambitions came into the open at the council of Constantinople in 381, the second ecumenical council to which, characteristically, Damasus I was not invited.

Here it was decreed that the bishop of Constantinople should hold the first rank after the bishop of Rome, 'because Constantinople is the new Rome'. The purpose, no doubt, was to give Constantinople an unassailable position in the east by placing it above Antioch and Alexandria, and Rome was not directly affected. But Damasus immediately reacted, and in 382 a Roman synod pronounced – with obvious reference to the decision of the previous year – that the Roman church owed its 'primacy' not to the decrees of a synod, but to the powers committed to Peter by Christ. Rome was 'the first see of the apostle Peter'; it was, indeed, the 'apostolic see' without qualification, and it is significant that Damasus was the first to appropriate the title 'apostolic' to Roman use, just as in his later letters he used the 'plural of majesty' and addressed bishops for the first time as 'sons', instead of 'brothers'. The pretensions of Constantinople had propelled Rome, with sudden force, along the road to primacy; they compelled it to gather together its earlier titles and combine them into a single claim to be 'the exclusive inheritor of all, and more than all, that the New Testament tells us of the prerogative of St Peter.'

The pontificate of Damasus I was, by common consent, a landmark in the history of the papacy. No doubt it would be easy to exaggerate its practical effects. Neither of the pope's great contemporaries, St Ambrose or St Augustine, shared his view of the consequences to be drawn from Christ's words to Peter. St Peter, Ambrose wrote, had 'a primacy of confession not of office, a primacy of faith not of rank.' But Damasus I's successors at Rome stubbornly maintained, if they did not necessarily develop, his view of the pope's special position. Siricius (384–99), the first Roman bishop to use the title 'pope', claimed for the pope's 'rescripts' or 'decretals' the same binding force as synodal decrees, since (he asserted) 'the care of all the churches' was 'committed to him'. Innocent I (401–17) maintained that all 'greater causes' (*causæ maiores*) – a vague and almost infinitely expansible expression – should be reserved to the apostolic see. 'Whatever is done in the provinces', he laid down, 'should not be taken as concluded until it has come to the knowledge of this see', adding that the pope's decisions affected 'all the churches of the world'. Here was a claim to universal authority, which Boniface I (418–22), stung into action by the attempts of Constantinople to interfere in Illyria, reiterated and strengthened. The Roman church, he said, stood to 'the churches throughout the world as the head is to its members.' Though bishops might hold 'one and the same episcopal office', they should 'recognize those to whom for the sake of ecclesiastical discipline they ought to be subject.'

10, 11 Allegorical representations of Rome and Constantinople, rival focal points
within the divided Roman empire; ivory reliefs of the second half of the fifth century

With these words Boniface foreshadowed the conception of Roman primacy to which Leo I's theory of the Petrine monarchy gave finality. That is not to say that the pope's claims were generally accepted. When Boniface's successor, Celestine I (422–32), sought to interfere in Africa, a council of African bishops at Carthage vigorously rejected his intervention, and when, at the council of Ephesus in 431, the pope's representative said that St Peter – by whom he meant the pope – was 'the head of the entire faith', the assembly made it plain that it was unwilling to endorse his claim. But by the time of Leo I (440–61) circumstances had changed; and it was this radical change in circumstances which made it possible for Leo to assert the primacy of Rome with an assurance and firmness without precedent in the past.

No doubt, Leo's personality also played a part. In spirit, if not by birth, a Roman of the Romans, by training an administrator, he brought to his office the inbred sense of authority of the Roman governing class and a strong admixture of traditional Roman pride. His tone and speech are those of a born ruler, and it is significant that he is the first pope to take over the old heathen title, *pontifex maximus*, which the emperors had discarded. But nothing is more characteristic of Leo than his emphasis on St Peter's princely authority. For him Peter is not only the 'prince of the apostles'; he is also a great prince of the church, who 'rightly rules all who are ruled in the first instance by Christ.' What is new in Leo's attitude is this emphasis on 'rule' and 'principality', culminating in the conception of the church as a monarchy ruled by the pope acting on Peter's behalf.

What made Leo's imperious attitude possible was the rapid decline of the empire. In the east, where the Nestorian controversy was raging, there was always one party at least which, even if only out of self-interest, was ready to turn to Rome, acknowledging, like bishop Theodoret of Cyrrhus, its 'hegemony over the churches of the world'. In the west, all was confusion as barbarian Germanic tribes, driven forward by the Huns, fanned out across the Roman provinces. Rome itself was sacked by Alaric in 410. By 442 Spain and North Africa were under the control of Visigoths and Vandals. In both countries the synodal organization collapsed, and the bishops who, only twenty years earlier, had resisted papal interference, turned willingly to the apostolic see for help and support. Leo was quick to grasp his opportunity, 'impelled' (he said) 'by that solicitude which, by divine institution, we bestow upon the universal church'. And the same unhappy sequence of events ensured him the backing of the imperial government, only too anxious to underwrite any authority which seemed able to hold the crumbling empire together. This was the origin of Valentinian III's famous decree of 455, supporting Leo against Hilary of Arles, who had asserted the independence of the church of Gaul, and instructing Aetius, the provincial governor, that, 'if any bishop summoned to trial before the bishop of Rome shall neglect to come,' he was to compel him to attend. This decree traditionally marks the establishment of the pope's primacy of jurisdiction and his unchallenged supremacy as patriarch of the west.

Leo also intervened actively in the doctrinal disputes raging in the east, and it was his definition of Christian dogma that prevailed at the council of Chalcedon in 451. But if this success – 'Peter has spoken through Leo !' – added immeasurably to the reputation of the holy see, the pope suffered a corresponding setback when the council, in its sixteenth session, decided that Constantinople was 'to enjoy the same primacy' in the east as Rome exercised in the west. Although veiled in placatory phrases designed to appease Leo, the decision of 451 went a long way beyond that of 381. Effectively it placed Rome and Constantinople on a level of parity; and this the pope could not accept. But he could not do anything about it either, and the rise of Constantinople continued, so much so that, by the time of pope Felix III (483–92), the patriarch of Constantinople was claiming to be 'prince of the whole church'. In the west Leo's claims may have been generally admitted; but in the east he was faced with deadlock.

Nevertheless Leo I made a capital contribution to the doctrine of papal primacy, and it is no accident that his letters and decretals found a prominent place in later canon law. It was Leo who first formulated the idea of the pope as the representative of Peter, 'cuius vice fungimur' – a phrase which succinctly summarizes the essence of papal claims and constantly recurs through future papal history. It was Leo, again, who first laid claim to the 'plenitude of power' which later played so decisive a role in the development of the papal monarchy. The hierarchical conception, according to which 'the cure of the universal church should converge towards Peter's one seat', owes more to him than to any other individual. Leo carried the papacy as far theoretically as it could go. But it was still part of the state church of the Empire, and the ambiguous relations of the bishop of Rome and the Roman emperor had not been resolved.

THE EMANCIPATION OF THE PAPACY

The history of the papacy after Leo I is often told as the story of the successive steps by which the bishop of Rome released himself from the authority of the Roman emperor. This picture of the popes straining at the leash,   27 cunningly 'making the best use of their opportunities in the interests of freeing the Roman church from its galling subjection to Constantinople', is, to say the least, grossly over-simplified. If in the course of the next three centuries the church of Rome gradually drew apart from the empire, it was the result of political developments for which the popes were in no way responsible, and which for the most part they actively deplored and re-sisted. Leo I himself was entirely loyal, his whole mentality that of a Roman in the universal empire. When, in the two best-remembered incidents of his whole career, he went out in 452 with a senatorial embassy to parley with the Huns and, three years later, attempted to persuade the Vandals to spare Rome, his action was undertaken quite as much on behalf of the empire as in the interests of the church.

Fifteen years after Leo's death, the barbarian flood, whose beginnings he had seen, engulfed the west. In 476 the emperor Zeno formally recognized the Vandal conquest of north Africa; the Visigoths were in firm control of Spain, while Burgundians and Franks were busy overrunning Gaul, and Italy was ruled by Odoacer until, in 493, he was ousted by the Goths under Theodoric. The consequences were as momentous for the church as for the state; and it would be more correct to see the history of the popes in the subsequent period, not as a struggle to emancipate themselves from the east, but rather as a desperate effort to keep their heads above water in the perplexities of a falling world.

It is unnecessary to follow in detail the complicated and often devious manœuvres in which this struggle involved them. So far as their limited means allowed, they played off one party against another, and occasionally the support of a barbarian ruler enabled them to assert a more independent position in their dealings with Constantinople. This was seen in the case of pope Gelasius I (492–96) who told the emperor – contrary to the whole practice of imperial government since Constantine – 'that bishops, not the secular power, should be responsible for the administration of the church', and laid down – in a statement which governed the relations of church and state for centuries to come – that the world was ruled by two powers, 'the sacred authority of the bishops' and the 'royal power', adding that, of the two, the former was the weightier, since the priests had to render account to God for kings. If Gelasius could take this firm line with Anastasius, it was because the Goths were in power in Italy and he could rely on Theodoric's protection. But this situation was exceptional. The effects of the barbarian invasions were almost as disastrous for the pope as for the emperor, and the western patriarchate, where previously – if grudgingly – his primacy had been recognized, had suffered a drastic shrinkage. Spain, North Africa and Italy were under Arian rulers, and did not recognize the ecclesiastical authority of Rome; and even in Gaul, where the heathen Franks had been converted to Catholicism, the affairs of the church were regulated by episcopal assemblies which resisted papal interference in organization and discipline. By the beginning of the sixth century, papal authority west of the Adriatic was confined, in effect, to central and southern Italy, and it is not surprising that the papacy clung to the empire as a sheet-anchor in a perilous sea of troubles. In any case, the reconquest of Italy by Justinian, which began in 533, left no practical alternative.

The re-establishment of imperial rule in Italy by Justinian marked the beginning of what Caspar has called the 'Byzantine period' in the history of the papacy. What this meant for the Roman church has already been briefly recounted. If the emperors from Zeno (474–91) to Constantine IV (668–85) put pressure both on Rome and Constantinople, they no doubt believed that they were justified by urgent political considerations, particularly the fear that incessant doctrinal controversies would result in the loss of the important provinces of Syria and Egypt. The fluctuations of policy which resulted may be passed over in silence. So far as the papacy was concerned, the result was to reduce the pope's moral authority in the west to the lowest ebb. When Vigilius surrendered to Justinian in the 'Three Chapters' controversy, the great sees of Milan, Ravenna and Aquileja rejected him, and even minor Sicilian bishops ignored the papacy for years on end. Constantinople, on the other hand, though often under greater pressure, was favoured as a more pliant tool. It was in the sixth century that the bishop of Constantinople began to use the title 'ecumenical' or 'universal patriarch', and Justinian himself, in one of his edicts, referred to Constantinople, without qualification, as 'the head of all other churches'. From the time of Pelagius I (555–61), the dependence of the papacy on the state was expressed in the practice – which continued until 741 – of sending the name of the elected pope, accompanied by a considerable payment, equivalent to a tribute, for confirmation either to the emperor himself in Constantinople or to his representative in Italy, the exarch of Ravenna. There appeared, one historian has written, 'to be no more room for the idea of Roman primacy', and the church of Rome seemed on the point of becoming a mere outpost of the Greek-speaking Roman empire, confronting the barbarian west, instead of an outpost of the west, as it actually became. Out of thirteen popes between 678 and 752 no less than eleven were Greeks or Syrians by birth.

What rescued the papacy, and ultimately turned its efforts in new directions, was the impact of two unforeseen events. The one was the descent of the Lombards into Italy in 568 and their expansion south towards Ravenna and Rome. The other was the victorious advance of a new religion, Islam, which, shortly after the death of its prophet, Mohammed, in 632, burst out of its Arabian homeland, overran Syria and Egypt, and turned against Byzantium itself in the east, and its North African provinces in the west.

The onslaught of Islam profoundly affected the position of the imperial government in Constantinople, forcing it to concentrate on the problems of its eastern frontier and limiting its capacity to interfere in the west. It also affected the position of the Roman church in a more direct way. The Mohammedan conquests, flooding over eastern Christendom, swept away the ancient rivals of the bishop of Rome, the patriarchates of Alexandria, Antioch and Jerusalem, as well as the church of Carthage, which in earlier centuries had been the great intellectual centre of the west, far outshining Rome. It is hardly too much to say, with Ferdinand Lot, that the triumph of Islam had the unintended and unexpected result 'of raising Rome to new heights through the ruin of the great cities of the east, the cradle of Christianity.' Rome, it is true, still had to face the rivalry of Constantinople and the pressure of the imperial government; and so long as the imperial administration in Italy, re-established by Justinian, remained effective, these were serious threats against which, in the long run, it might have been difficult for the Roman bishop to hold out. But here the entry on the scene of the Lombards brought decisive changes.

It would, of course, be wrong to suggest that the arrival of the Lombards in Italy resulted in an immediate transformation of the relations of empire and papacy. On the contrary, the very existence of this new threat was an inducement for the bishop of Rome to hold firm to the imperial connection. Nothing is more remarkable than the loyalty of the papacy to the empire, long after the empire had ceased to provide effective support. In spite of the violent doctrinal controversies which broke out in the eighth century, it was pope Gregory II (715–31), a Roman, who brought the revolt to heel when rebellion broke out in Italy in 727 and 728. Even Stephen II (752–57), who summoned in the Franks, was no less loyal to the empire than his predecessors. If he turned to the Frankish ruler Pippin, it was only because his request for help from Constantinople had been ignored. The popes might stand out against the emperor on questions of dogma and resist the pretensions of the patriarch of Constantinople; but politically they were loyal. In

12 The earliest known representation of Gregory I, often hailed as 'the first of the medieval popes'; monk, writer, diplomat, administrator and moral leader

part, no doubt, this was because they simply could not afford to dispense with imperial support, if they could get it; but more fundamentally it was because, in his own eyes, the bishop of Rome was still, first and foremost, the first bishop of the empire, the *imperium Christianum* which was the very heart of Christendom.

This is nowhere clearer than in the attitude of Gregory I (590–604), the first of the popes directly confronted, at the very gates of Rome, by the Lombard peril. It is still usual to see Gregory, largely on account of the mission he dispatched to England in 596, as the first pope who deliberately set out to cultivate new fields, outside and beyond the control of the Roman empire, and thus to lessen the dependence of the papacy on the imperial government. This is not true. The propagation of Christianity, not the extension of his own sphere of authority, was Gregory's object when he undertook the conversion of the Anglo-Saxons; a monk himself – the first

31

monk to ascend the throne of St Peter – his motives were genuinely religious, not political. Nor is there any sign, in his relations with the imperial government, of a desire to modify the existing situation. Like Leo I before him, like his own immediate predecessor, Pelagius II (579–90), he firmly resisted the pretensions of the bishop of Constantinople, replying to the latter's assumption of the title 'universal patriarch' not (as might be expected) by asserting his own universal authority as successor of St Peter, but by the argument – equally destructive of any claims the papacy might make – that none of the patriarchs could claim to be universal. For his own part, Gregory described himself simply as 'servant of God's servants' – a happy formula which from his day forward became a regular part of the pope's official title. But towards the empire his attitude was one of unquestioning loyalty, almost of religious reverence, so much so that he has frequently been censured for his subservience to the despicable tyrant, Phocas. Precisely because he was so aware of the perils of the times, the ever-present fear of death and the vanity of worldly hope, he had no ambition to extend the power of the Roman church; and the old view of Gregory, which sees him first and foremost as the founder of the temporal power of the papacy and the first of a series of political popes leading through Gregory VII and Innocent III to Boniface VIII, takes too little account of these facts.

Nevertheless, even in Gregory's day and increasingly thereafter, conditions were imperceptibly changing, and these changes necessarily affected the pope's position. For one thing, the Lombards inevitably had first claim on the attention and resources of the exarch at Ravenna, and the situation at Rome took second place. In addition, the existence of the Lombard duchy of Spoleto, driven like a wedge between Ravenna and Rome, isolated the pope and made it less easy to bring pressure to bear on him. With the collapse of the old civil administration under the emperor Maurice (582–602), the duchy of Rome began to go its own way. In Rome, as in other cities, the bishop was now the main surviving civilian dignitary, and his officials, appointed originally to superintend church affairs, almost of necessity took over functions, such as the maintenance of water supplies and provision for the poor and needy, which hitherto had been performed by the civil authority. Furthermore, the church of Rome by now had great resources at its disposal. Pelagius I had began the reorganization of its estates, ruined during Justinian's wars against the Goths. Gregory I carried his work to completion, considerably increasing the revenues from the so-called 'patrimony of St Peter'. The papacy was already – though the fact was not yet formally recognized – a territorial power, and this enabled the pope to act with new strength and freedom. It was the bishop of Rome who now took care of the provisioning of the city, importing corn from Sicily; it was Gregory himself who, in the crises of 591 and 593, used the church's resources to buy off the Lombards; and soon it was the pope who paid the troops of the Roman duchy, who not unnaturally, since their salaries came from the papal treasury, began to look to him as their head. In a letter to the empress Constantina, Gregory described himself succinctly as 'paymaster' of Rome, on a par with the emperor's paymaster in Ravenna. When the Lombards appeared before the walls of Rome, it was Gregory who – in spite of instructions to the contrary from the government in Constantinople – negotiated a separate peace.

There is no doubt that this diplomatic activity raised the pope's prestige, just as his moral leadership won him the regard of the Roman populace. Throughout the Lombard crisis he acted not as the representative of the emperor, bound by imperial instructions, but as an independent third party. It was not that he was disloyal to the empire, but simply that the Italian provinces, which the imperial government was unable to look after properly, were beginning to go their own way. Moreover, his negotiations with the Lombard ruler, Agilulf, brought Gregory into direct relations with the nations outside the Roman empire. Here again, sheer necessity, rather than policy, dictated his actions; he could not simply ignore a people living on his doorstep. But it certainly opened up new perspectives. Just as Gregory felt it his duty to convert the heathen Anglo-Saxons to Christianity, so it was an obvious step, for a man of his essentially religious outlook, to convert the Arian Lombards to Catholicism. He also sought to re-establish the old links with the church in Spain, where the Visigothic rulers had recently abandoned Arianism, and to interest the Frankish rulers in the reform of the corrupt and dissolute church in Gaul. None of these endeavours had much success. In England, the missionary work of Augustine was undone in the heathen reaction after the death of Ethelbert of Kent in 616, and more than half a century passed before, in the days of Theodore of Tarsus, the lost ground was recovered. It was to Theodore of Tarsus, archbishop of Canterbury from 669 to 690, and not to Augustine, that the church in England owed its unity, its organization, and the influence it exerted in the following century over the destinies of western Christendom.

Nevertheless, the pontificate of Gregory I marked the beginning of new developments, and it is for this reason that he has so often been hailed – not very convincingly – as 'the first of the medieval popes'. From Gregory's time forward the changing situation made it increasingly difficult to maintain the fiction of one Christian church in one Christian empire. So long as the emperor retained any semblance of authority in the western Mediterranean, the church felt itself to be naturally allied with the empire. When his hold over Africa, Spain and Italy relaxed, it was compelled to make its own compromises with the barbarian rulers of the west. If Gregory I himself was not conscious of the change which had occurred, this was because it was not until after the middle of the seventh century, when the Arab fleet controlled the Mediterranean and the Slavs had cut the land route from Constantinople to the west, that the consequences became obvious; but the change was nevertheless real. And it was reinforced and consolidated by other changes of a more general character. East and west were drifting apart. The reforms of the emperor Heraclius, who came to power in 610, six years after Gregory's death, accentuated the Greek, or Hellenistic, character of the empire. The language difference, which reached back at least to the end of the fourth century, was becoming more marked. Gregory I himself could speak no Greek, and showed something like disdain for the Greek tongue. And with differences of language went differences of doctrine and thought. Already in the time of Justinian the churches of the Latin west – Italy, Africa, Spain and Gaul – united to resist his attempt to force them to accept Greek doctrines. And finally, as the seventh century progressed, and sea-borne trade decreased, there was a noticeable slackening in commercial and administrative contacts between east and west. The last emperor actually to visit Rome was Constans II in 663, and this was after an interlude of almost two centuries. The last pope to visit Constantinople was Constantine I in 710.

It would be easy to write as though the changes visible at the time of Gregory I's death led by inexorable steps to the emancipation of the papacy from the empire. That is not the case. It needed another crisis – or rather another series of crises – before the decisive steps were taken; and this did not occur until the eighth century. For one thing, the situation in Italy became more stable, as the Lombard rulers consolidated their hold, and more particularly after their conversion to Catholicism, which was completed about 680. For another, the attitude of the imperial government in Constantinople became more accommodating. That it was still perilous for the pope to oppose the emperor's doctrinal policy was shown by the fate of Martin I (649–55), who was arrested and banished to the Crimea, where he died after great suffering in 655. But once the emperor gave up hope of reconquering Syria and Egypt, which had fallen to the Arabs in

640 and 642, there was no further need to placate his Monophysite subjects; and his attitude changed. Realizing the danger of alienating his few remaining provinces in the west, where discontent was rife, Constantine IV sought a reconciliation; and in 681 the sixth ecumenical council at Constantinople endorsed the papal definition of the nature of Christ and brought the long Christological conflict to an end. It was a victory, though a mixed victory, for Rome.

Two independent, but decisive, events destroyed the uneasy peace which followed, and precipitated the final crisis. The one was the action of Leo III, the first emperor of the new Isaurian dynasty, in stirring up a new theological controversy by attacking the worship of images. The other was the renewal, after more than half a century, of the Lombard advance. The causes of the iconoclastic controversy, the opening shots of which were fired by Leo in 726, do not concern us here. Its result was revolution in Italy, a breach between Gregory II (715–31) and the emperor, and the beginning of the longest and bitterest schism between east and west which the church had so far experienced. When Gregory II's successor, a Syrian who took the name Gregory III (731–41), refused to come to heel, Leo proceeded to more drastic measures. First, he confiscated the papal estates in Sicily and southern Italy, from which, as we know, the bulk of the pope's income was derived; and simultaneously, or nearly simultaneously, he undertook a major reorganization of the imperial church. At one stroke, the Greek-speaking provinces of Illyria, Sicily and southern Italy – in other words, the archbishoprics of Thessalonica, Corinth, Syracuse, Reggio, Nicopolis, Athens and Patras – which had hitherto been under the pope's jurisdiction, were taken away and placed under the patriarch of Constantinople. It would be hard to exaggerate the importance of this revolutionary measure, which occurred, apparently, in 732 or 733. For the papacy it meant, in Caspar's words, 'the final destruction of the world in which it had risen.' For all practical purposes, it was cut off from the imperial church, of which it had hitherto regarded itself as the head, and reduced to an outlying see with authority over little more than the neighbouring, so-called 'suburbicarian' bishoprics. Far from seeking to liberate itself from the empire, it had, in effect, been thrown out of the empire, or at least put into quarantine on the outer periphery.

Though Leo III's iconoclastic policy had such momentous consequences for the papacy, the reasons he embarked on it had nothing to do with the west or Italy, and its results were unintentional. The same is true of the second decisive factor in the situation, the renewal of the Lombard advance.

This began under Liutprand (712–44), a pious Christian, well disposed to the church, whose object was not to bring Rome into subjection, but to extend his authority over the two Lombard duchies in the south, Spoleto and Benevento. But this policy, if only for reasons of geography, could hardly help embroiling him and his successors, Ratchis (744–49) and Aistulf (749–56), with the imperial administration in Ravenna and with the pope in Rome, since it was almost impossible to control Spoleto and Benevento without some readjustment of frontiers. It may be true, as Duchesne once wrote, that the papacy 'had little to lose by passing from Byzantine to Lombard rule'. But Byzantine rule in Rome was now little more than nominal; the pope was almost autonomous, negotiating separately with the Lombard dukes and king; and if the whole Italian peninsula passed under Lombard control, his independence, which was a product of the balance between the imperial and Lombard forces, was bound to suffer.

Hence the year 739, when Liutprand for the first time occupied Ravenna and drove out the exarch, was a turning-point for the papacy. In vain Gregory III begged the Frankish ruler, Charles Martel, to intervene. Finally, Gregory's successor, pope Zacharias (741–52), saved the situation by some deft manœuvres, but only temporarily. With the accession of Aistulf in 749 the Lombard monarchy revived its 'forward' policy. In 751 Ravenna again fell, this time definitively, and Aistulf pressed forward to the walls of Rome, imposed a heavy tribute on the inhabitants of the Roman duchy in token of subjection, and placed the duchy under his jurisdiction.

At this critical juncture the Greek pope, Zacharias, died; and for the first time in twenty-one years a Roman was elected in his place. This was Stephen II (752–57). The election of a Roman was a consequence of the critical situation; it was necessary to have someone experienced in local conditions who could cope with the gathering storm. But what was to be done? Stephen II was no less loyal to the empire than his predecessors. But the iconoclastic controversy was at its height – at the beginning of 754 a great synod in Constantinople, attended by no less than 338 bishops, launched the most vehement of all attacks on image-worshippers – and in any case the emperor could do nothing. Stephen made repeated calls for help. Then, realizing that nothing was to be expected, he sent, like Gregory III before him, a petition to the Frankish ruler. This time the call was answered. After a fruitless interview with Aistulf at Pavia, Stephen set out on 15 November 753 for the Frankish kingdom. Here, early in 754, the Frankish king, Pippin, and Stephen met. The pope, on his knees and in tears, besought Pippin's protection. Pippin, for his part, promised to defend and protect the rights of St Peter. The connection between the papacy and the Frankish monarchy, which was so decisively to affect papal history for the next five centuries, had been forged.

In 754 the long-term consequences could not, of course, be foreseen. The link with the Frankish kingdom might have been a flash in the pan, like other manœuvres in the game of checks and balances the Roman bishop had become accustomed to playing. The connection with Byzantium, troubled and tenuous as it now was, was still maintained, and for another half-century the course of events hung in the balance. The Byzantine period in the history of the papacy did not end suddenly in 754. It did not even end in 800, when pope Leo III crowned the Frankish king, Charles the Great, as emperor. Most popes of the ninth century – most notably of all, pope John VIII (872–82) – looked over one shoulder at the empire in the east; and right down to the turn of the tenth and eleventh centuries, when Byzantium had risen to new heights under Basil II (976–1025), there were contacts between the pope in Rome and the imperial court in Constantinople.

Old habits die hard. But the pontificate of Stephen II may nevertheless be taken as the end of an epoch in the history of the papacy. What was decisive was the pressure of events. This inexorable pressure, rather than any positive decision on the part of the pope, enforced a change of orientation which proved irreversible. From the moment of its recognition under Constantine the papacy had moved in a Roman or imperial, and therewith in an eastern, sphere. Since Gregory the Great it had hovered on the edge of two worlds. After 754 it went over into a western orbit. It carried with it much from its past, particularly the Petrine tradition to which it had clung so stubbornly, and its claim to primacy over the churches of the west; but it was only after 754, in a new environment, that it acquired the authority which enabled it to play so significant a role in the future history of Europe.

13 The 'Donation of Constantine'. This twelfth-century fresco shows the emperor
Constantine conferring dominion over Rome on pope Sylvester I (314–35) – the
subject of a famous eighth-century forgery

II THE RISE OF THE MEDIEVAL PAPACY

Few incidents in the history of the papacy have been more fully discussed than the meeting between Stephen II and Pippin at Ponthion on 6 January 754. What exactly did the pope expect of Pippin? With what plans of his own had he journeyed to the Frankish court? How did he view the future of the church of Rome?

Since the documentary evidence is fragmentary, obscure, and in many places suspect, all answers to these questions are speculative. But, among a mass of speculation, one or two facts are clear. In the first place, it is evident that originally Stephen simply requested Pippin to arrange matters 'peacefully' – in other words, to use his influence with the Lombard king. And it was in the same spirit that Pippin responded. Three embassies were sent to Aistulf, asking him, reasonably and moderately, to abstain from hostilities in the neighbourhood of Rome out of respect for St Peter and St Paul. Only when these appeals produced no effect did Pippin go further. This was at an assembly at Quierzy in mid-April, where it was decided to use force, if necessary. And at Quierzy, also, another event occurred, of great historical importance. This was a solemn engagement on Pippin's part to hand over, or restore, extensive territories in Italy to the pope. There is, it is true, no contemporary record of Pippin's promise; but if we are to believe a report some twenty years later in date – as most historians do – it included the whole of the exarchate of Ravenna, the duchies of Spoleto and Benevento, the provinces of Venice and Istria and the southern part of the Lombard kingdom – more than half, in short, of the Italian peninsula.

The 'Donation of Quierzy', as it is called, casts a good deal of light, if only obliquely, on the pope's ideas and intentions. Furthermore, it does not stand alone. There is, for example, much talk, at least in papal sources, of the 'Roman republic', also (an almost untranslatable phrase) of the *sanctæ Dei ecclesiæ respublica*, which is meant perhaps – it is almost the only conceivable meaning – to imply an autonomous Roman duchy governed by, or at least closely dependent on, the pope. And this may be why the pope conferred on Pippin and his sons – though Pippin was careful never to use it – a new-fangled title *patricius Romanorum*, which perhaps indicates that he

39

wished to regard him as the protector of the new 'republic'. None of these things are certain, and we must be careful, in this strange world of legend and superstition and half-understood imperial phraseology, not to read too much into a few ambiguous words. But cumulatively they suggest that something new was in the air and that the pope, knowing full well that the situation in Italy was too unstable to last, had made up his mind, once he was assured of Frankish help, that more than a mere restoration of the *status quo* was necessary.

The most circumstantial evidence for this is the famous forgery, the so-called 'Donation of Constantine', according to which – among many other things, including confirmation of the pope's primacy over the four patri-archates of the east – the emperor Constantine, on transferring the capital of the empire to Constantinople in 326, handed over to pope Sylvester I domi-nion over 'the city of Rome and all the places, cities and provinces of Italy and the west'. The date of this famous forgery is not known. It may have been put together under Stephen II himself, perhaps about 756, or under his successor and brother, Paul I (757–67); many historians attribute it to 774, and a recent investigation has suggested that it was added to, piece by piece, at different stages between 754 and 796. But it can scarcely be denied (though a number of historians have done so) that it reflects the situation which existed in the second half of the eighth century. Taking the evidence as a whole, it seems clear that the pope had decided that he would only be safe, after the imperial government had been expelled from Ravenna in 751, if he stepped into the exarch's place as ruler of imperial Italy, and if, at the same time, the Lombard kingdom were reduced to its original dimensions, roughly as it was a century and a half earlier, immediately after the Lombard invasion.

It was, considering all the obstacles, a plan of the utmost audacity; but it is difficult to explain the facts on any other hypothesis. And not its least audacious aspect was the claim it embodied to temporal rule. Such a claim was quite unprecedented. At no time in the whole preceding history of the papacy had there been any suggestion that the bishop of Rome should exer-cise temporal power, or rule like a king over a territorial state. If this claim was now made, it was, no doubt, in response to a peculiarly difficult situa-tion. But the claim, once made, was never dropped. It runs like a red thread through papal history right down to the Lateran treaties of 1929, and for long periods in the middle ages, particularly between the pontificate of Alexander III (1159–81) and the Reformation, it played an important part in papal policy and influenced the very character of the papacy itself. The claim to temporal power, and the attempt to exercise political control over the 'lands' or 'patrimony of St Peter', is one of the clearest signs that the history of the papacy had entered a new period.

At first, and for a period of roughly twenty years, it looked as if this revolutionary plan would miraculously succeed. While the Frankish army was gathering, Pippin sent one final appeal to Aistulf. When this was ignored, Frankish troops crossed the Alps, and won a decisive victory. In October 754 Aistulf capitulated, acknowledged Frankish overlordship, and promised in a solemn charter to hand over his conquests, the exarchate and the frontier fortresses of the Roman duchy, to St Peter. But, much to the pope's chagrin, Pippin exacted no guarantees, and when the Frankish army returned home, Aistulf went back on his promise; at the beginning of 756 a new army, which he sent against Rome, beseiged the city for eight weeks. Once again, urgent appeals went out to Pippin – this time St Peter himself, 'standing before you, living, in the flesh', was called in to cajole and threaten the unfortunate king – and this time more effective measures were taken. Aistulf was again compelled to recognize Pippin's overlordship, and commissioners, backed by armed forces, were sent out to supervise the transfer

14 The capitulation of Aistulf, king of the Lombards, to pope Stephen II; from a twelfth-century manuscript

of the surrendered territories – the exarchate of Ravenna and those parts of the duchy of Rome which Aistulf had conquered – to the pope. An embassy which arrived post-haste from Constantinople protested that the exarchate was imperial territory. Pippin's reply, in effect, was that he had conquered it from the Lombards and had no intention of restoring it to the emperor; he had only engaged in war for love of St Peter and for the remission of his sins, and to St Peter the profits were to go.

In this way, the 'papal state' (as it was later to be called) came into existence. Byzantium, or the Roman empire, was finally excluded, though it did not, of course, surrender the hope of recovering its Italian province and, from its base in Sicily and the south, which remained Byzantine until the eleventh century, it continued to play an active part in Italian politics. But in other respects it was at the moment of triumph in 756 that the pope's real difficulties began. In the first place, there was the difficulty – which dogged papal history right down to the Renaissance – of making the pope's authority effective in the territories he had acquired; and this soon proved to be far beyond his capacity. In the outlying regions, northwards towards Bologna, papal rule was at best nominal, and in Ravenna itself it was the archbishop – a bitter opponent of the pretensions of the bishop of Rome – who actually profited. But even in the immediate vicinity of Rome, the Campagna and the Sabine hills, the reality of power was in the hands of the wealthy landowners, and as early as 757 there occurred the first struggles among the different aristocratic factions to control and nominate the pope, a foreshadowing of the dismal fate which overtook the papacy in the tenth and early eleventh centuries. But these problems, serious as they were, were not the only ones. In addition, the papacy had to cope with the Franks and the Lombards. It was not to be supposed that the latter would meekly accept their defeat; but how long would the Franks go on underwriting the pope's position without demanding anything in return except the privilege of being in St Peter's good books? The death of Aistulf in 756, of Stephen II in 757 and finally of Pippin himself in 768, brought all these problems to a head.

15 The political geography of Italy in the seventh and eighth centuries was unusually complicated. The map shows the division between imperial and Lombard Italy and the lands claimed by the papacy on the basis of the Donation of Pippin. It was particularly important for the development of the papal states that the connection between the exarchate of Ravenna and the duchy of Rome was almost severed by the Lombard duchy of Spoleto, and that the Lombard king, with his seat in Pavia, could only extend his authority over the duchy of Spoleto by encroaching on imperial territory

▶

At first it seemed that all was well. On Aistulf's death the succession to the Lombard crown was disputed, and the successful claimant, Desiderius, to get the pope's support, offered to hand over the conquests of Liutprand. It seemed as if, step by step, the papal programme was being realized. But once again the Lombard promises were not fulfilled, and this time Pippin did not intervene. Perhaps he was prevented by wars in Aquitaine; more likely, he calculated that he had fulfilled his promises and had no obligation to help the papacy to extend its possessions beyond the terms of the settlement of 756. His object now was to keep the peace between the pope – he was Stephen II's brother, Paul I (757–67) – and Desiderius. His earlier intervention had been based on religious, not on political grounds, and he had no quarrel with the Lombards. Perhaps already he was thinking of a return to the Lombard alliance of his father's day. Certainly that is what occurred after his death in 768, and the pontificate of Stephen III (768–72), when this Franco-Lombard *rapprochement* was at its height, was an anxious time for

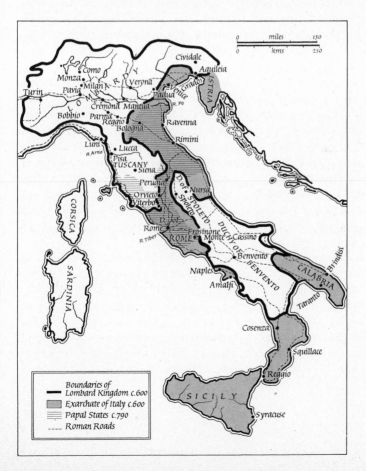

the papacy. It was only when a new pope, Hadrian I (772–95), and a new Frankish king, Charles the Great (768–814) came on the scene that the Lombard question was settled. What made Charles reverse the pro-Lombard alignment when he became sole ruler at the end of 771, we do not need to inquire; but the results were decisive. In 773 Charles invaded Italy and this time there was no thought of a distant overlordship. Desiderius was deposed, and in 774 Charles himself became king of the Lombards. A few weeks earlier, on a visit to Rome, he had solemnly renewed Pippin's promises of 754.

But now the situation had changed. It was one thing for Pippin to intervene as a religious duty, quite another to have Charles established in Italy on a permanent footing. Once Charles became king of the Lombards, the divergence between his interests and those of the pope became increasingly apparent. Why, in particular, should he dismember his newly acquired kingdom for the pope's benefit? In fact, Charles was so slow to carry out his promises that Hadrian bitterly – and incorrectly – complained that none of Pippin's undertakings had been fulfilled. When Charles was called to Italy a second time in 776 to put down a Lombard rebellion, he left without visiting Rome or doing anything to meet the pope's demands. Only on his third visit in 781 was anything settled, and then Hadrian had to make major concessions. A little more was obtained in 787; but by now it was obvious that the papal ambitions of 754 and 774 were not going to be fulfilled. The pope's position in the duchy of Rome was unquestioned, and its frontiers were extended a little to the north, approximately to Orvieto, and a little to the south, though here without permanent effects. Its boundaries were, in fact, roughly those of the papal states as they continued down to 1860. But outside this small domain, little remained of the ambitious plans of Stephen II. The claim to the duchies of Spoleto and Tuscany was given up, and even in the exarchate the pope had to meet the challenge of the archbishop of Ravenna, whose strivings for autonomy had Charles's support.

But the disappointment of the pope's territorial ambitions – of the plan (if such it was) to ensure the independence of the papacy by securing it an independent territorial position between the contending powers – was only the beginning. The longer Charles lived, and the further he extended his dominions, the more imperious he became. Charles's conception of his position in the church left scarcely more room than that of emperors such as Justinian for an independent papacy. Charles had no doubt about his vocation. Like Constantine the Great and his successors, he regarded himself

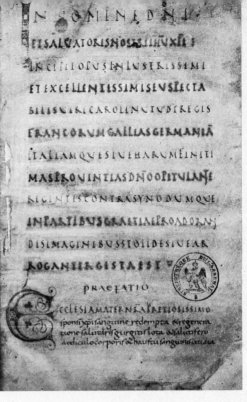

16, 17 The division of temporal and spiritual power: St Peter with pope Leo III and Charlemagne; watercolour copy of a lost ninth-century mosaic in the Lateran. Right, first page of the *Libri Carolini*, prepared under Charlemagne's instructions, to refute the council of Nicaea and assert his authority in matters of faith

as guardian of the faith – even against the pope, if need be – and lord over the church. He it was whom (in Alcuin's words) 'the dispensation of our Lord Jesus has made rector of the Christian people'; on him rested 'the whole salvation' – note the word 'whole' ! – 'of the Church of Christ.' He was, Alcuin said, more excellent in power than the other two dignitaries of the Christian world, the pope and the emperor, more distinguished in wisdom, more sublime in his royal dignity.

These were exalted claims, but Charles showed in his practice that he intended them to be a reality, and that he was not prepared to leave even matters of faith to the pope. When Rome and Constantinople came together in 787 to settle the iconoclastic dispute, Charles was outraged. His theologians were put to work to prepare a counterblast, the so-called *Libri Carolini*, and in 794 a synod met at Frankfurt with the express object of undoing the work of the seventh ecumenical council at Nicaea. Characteristically, Charles presided in person at Frankfurt, and the pope was forced, through his legates, to eat his words. There were even rumours that Charles intended to depose Hadrian and replace him by a Frankish prelate.

45

No wonder that, on Hadrian's death in 795, one party in Rome decided that it would be wise to elect a more submissive and less scrupulous pope than Hadrian had been. Leo III (795–816), a shadowy and faintly disreputable figure, was dependent throughout his pontificate on Frankish support, and Charles immediately put him in his place. It was for the ruler, Charles told him immediately after his accession, to protect the church from its enemies outside the gate and safeguard the Christian faith within; the pope's business was to help him in this task by prayer.

By 795, therefore, it was all too evident that the complicated manœuvres engaged in by the papacy since 754 had misfired. The papal state (as it was later to be called) had, indeed, been constructed, though within far narrower limits than either Stephen II or Hadrian I had envisaged. But even here papal authority fell far short of sovereignty. The most Charles was willing to concede was a limited autonomy under his own supreme overlordship, and the position of Rome and the Roman duchy remained ambiguous for centuries to come, a frequent source of conflict between empire and papacy. For the rest, it was painfully obvious that, in calling in the Franks, the pope had only changed one master for another. The pope was, indeed, the representative of St Peter; but Charles (as the Anglo-Saxon scholar, Cathwulf, told him) was the vicar of God. His religion was genuine, and permeated with the Roman spirit. It meant rigorous conformity, from the pope as from others, with the usages of the Roman church; and in this veneration for Rome as the source of true religion, Charles was typical of his day. But he had also no intention of abandoning one jot or tittle of the rights over the church the Roman emperors had exercised. It may be an exaggeration to say, as one historian has done, that never 'since the days of Justinian had the papacy sunk so low.' But that it was subordinate to the king, both in practice and in Charles's concept of his royal office, is certain. The pope was in no sense a negligible quantity, a mere figure-head. Charles wished to live in concord with him, and laid great store on his benediction. But he was, in Duchesne's happy phrase, 'the high priest of the Roman pilgrimage' and of the 'Roman sanctuaries', not a ruler either of state or of church.

THE WESTERN PEOPLES AND ROME

If the result of the events of the second half of the eighth century had only been to substitute the Frankish king for the Greek emperor, they would certainly not have marked a turning-point in the history of the papacy. But that was not the case. Politically, the papacy in 795 was hardly better placed than it had been in 754; but in turning away from the east and establishing new contacts with the west, it tapped new sources of moral strength. It did so unwittingly and with no inkling of the consequences; but the result, though it was slow to take effect, was to set the papacy off along new roads. For the attitude of the peoples of western Europe to the see of Rome was essentially different from that of the Mediterranean peoples among whom it had risen. For the latter the bishop of Rome was an exalted dignitary in the ecclesiastical hierarchy of the empire, perhaps the most exalted of all, a judge among bishops, an authority to be appealed to in theological disputes. For the former he was a religious figure of transcendental stature, important not for his place in the hierarchy, but because, as St Peter's successor, he could open or lock the gates of heaven, ease the way of the penitent sinner or damn the recalcitrant with eternal anathemas.

What this change of attitude signified was seen in Pippin's response to Stephen II in 754. When Pippin decided to intervene in Italy, it was a question not of political interest but of religious duty, and specifically of duty towards St Peter. In Stephen's letters to Pippin and the Frankish nobility, all the emphasis falls on Peter, the prince of the apostles, who will repay their efforts a hundredfold and assure them a place for all time in paradise. And it was in this spirit, as we have seen, that Pippin responded, seeking nothing for himself but only to restore to St Peter what was his. Nor was Pippin's attitude in any way unique. Liutprand, the Lombard king, had acted in the same way in 743, when he restored four strongholds on the frontier of the duchy of Rome which he had occupied on one of his expeditions against the duke of Spoleto. Like Pippin later, he gave them back specifically to St Peter, and out of reverence for St Peter; and in token of peace, he laid his weapons on St Peter's tomb.

This heart-felt devotion to St Peter, which extended to his successor, who spoke for him and through whom he spoke, was characteristic of all the newly converted peoples of western Europe. It accounts for the crowds of pilgrims who, beginning about the last quarter of the seventh century, made their way to Rome from Anglo-Saxon England in ever increasing numbers. But nowhere is the new attitude more graphically illustrated than in the famous scene at Whitby in 664, when king Oswiu of Northumbria was called upon to decide between the Roman and the Celtic ways of computing Easter. The Celts relied on the authority of St Columba; their opponents replied by citing that of St Peter, to whom Christ had given the keys of heaven. The question was whether Columba enjoyed similar powers, and when the Celts admitted that he did not, Oswiu made his

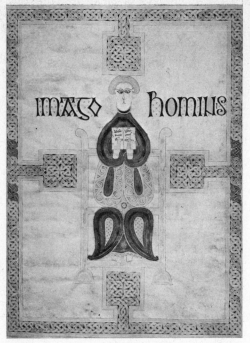

IMAGO hOMINIS

18 Miniature from the *Psalter of Echternach*, written in Northumbria at the end of the seventh century, which probably came to Echternach as the gift of St Willibrord on the occasion of the founding of the monastery in 698

19 This miniature from an eleventh-century sacramentary shows St Boniface baptizing the heathen and his martyrdom in 754 ▶

famous decision: 'Since Peter is the door-keeper, I will not resist him, but will follow him as best I can, so that, when I come to the gates of heaven, there will be someone there to open them for me and he who has the key will not turn me back.'

This veneration for St Peter, so characteristic of Anglo-Saxon England, betokened a new attitude towards Rome, the Roman church and the bishop of Rome, and missionaries from England carried it with them wherever they went. The story of the great Anglo-Saxon missions of the eighth century can only be briefly recounted. Their results nevertheless were of capital importance for the papacy. They began in 690 when St Willibrord set forth to convert the Frisians who inhabited the marshy lands along the coast near the mouth of the Rhine. They were continued by Wynfrith, who took the name Boniface – by which he is known in history – when pope Gregory II authorized his mission in 719. Boniface's main field of activity was central Germany, the land of the Hessians and Thuringians, but in 739 he moved into Bavaria, linking it up with the new religious centres he had established farther west.

By 741 the church in Germany was organized, and Boniface was free to turn his attention to the Frankish church, the discipline and organization of which had collapsed in the anarchy of the preceding century. Great reform synods were summoned, first in 742 and 743 for the eastern half of the kingdom, then in 744 for the west, and finally in 745 and 747 for the whole Frankish realm. By the time of Boniface's death in 754 the whole character of western Christendom had been transformed; the influence of the reformed Frankish church extended through Mainz and Eichstätt across Bavaria to Salzburg; and the whole was linked as never before with Rome. It was an extraordinary accession to the papacy's sphere of authority, an immense increase in the number of those who looked to Rome as the source of true religion and to the pope as its appointed guardian and exponent.

Both Willibrord and Boniface worked throughout in close connection with Rome. Both sought and received from the pope the *pallium*, which conferred archiepiscopal authority and entitled them to set up bishops in the newly converted lands. Boniface took an oath of obedience to St Peter and his successor, liked to call himself 'the legate of the holy see in Germany', and in 742 was succinctly addressed as 'St Peter's envoy'. And the synod of 747 sent a formal letter to Rome, signed by all the bishops present, declaring 'that we will maintain . . . subjection to the Roman see until the end of our lives' and 'desire in all things to follow the precepts of St Peter . . . so that we may be counted among the sheep entrusted to him.' This was a significant change. Before Boniface's reforms the pope's influence over the Frankish church had been negligible and it would be impossible to find a similar profession by a Merovingian synod. The immediate effects were nevertheless not great. It was Charles Martel's sons, Carloman and Pippin, who had initiated the reforms, and they had no intention of abdicating control. To begin with, therefore, the reform of the Frankish church made it a pillar of the Frankish monarchy, rather than an instrument of the bishop of Rome; and this remained the position down to the death of Pippin's son, Charles the Great, in 814.

When Alcuin wrote to Charles: 'May the ruler of the church be rightly ruled by thee, O king, and mayest thou be ruled by the right hand of the Almighty', his words were a faithful echo of the views current among Frankish churchmen at the close of the eighth century. Only when this conception of the relations of state and church had broken down under the stress of anarchy and civil war, did the inherent strength of the pope's position become evident. Meanwhile, the area which looked to Rome for spiritual direction was steadily expanding. The work of St Willibrord in the Netherlands and of St Boniface in Germany was only the beginning of a missionary movement which widened the basis of papal authority and put the papacy in possession of resources earlier popes had not even dreamed of. We can only summarize briefly the course of the subsequent missions: the conversion of the Saxons of north Germany, where Bremen was established in 787 as a missionary bishopric under the Anglo-Saxon, Willihad; the mission to the Slavs and Avars on the eastern and south-eastern confines of Bavaria, in whose conversion Salzburg, raised to a metropolitan see in 798, and Passau played a leading part; and in 831 the establishment of Hamburg as a missionary centre for the north. None of this occurred without setbacks. The conversion of the Saxons took thirty years and more, and was only effected by force, and Hamburg was overrun by the Vikings in 845. But slow and halting as it was, the Christianization of the Scandinavian north gradually took effect, and may be said to have been accomplished by the time of St Olaf of Norway (1015–31). At the same time king Stephen of Hungary (997–1038) accepted Christianity and entered into communion with Rome, rejecting missions from the Greek church in Byzantium; and both Bohemia, which had emerged as a stable state under Boleslav I (929–67), and Poland under Mieszko I (963–92) and Boleslav Chobry (992–1025) sought to forge direct links with Rome.

By the beginning of the eleventh century, therefore, the papacy had laid up a considerable store of moral capital. The new nations, the peoples whom Christianity had brought into the main current of European civilization, looked to Rome for spiritual leadership. It was a capital which lay fallow, accruing and accumulating almost unnoticed until new impulses reached Rome from north of the Alps in the course of the eleventh century. But when, under Gregory VII (1073–85), the need came to use it, its inherent potentialities were immediately apparent. It was no accident that, during Gregory VII's great conflict with the emperor Henry IV, he was able to draw on support from the countries on the periphery of the empire: Denmark, Poland, Hungary, Bohemia, Croatia. The work begun by St Boniface and his fellow Anglo-Saxons, with the support of the Frankish monarchy, had borne good fruit. Through their efforts, Latin Christendom had gradually taken shape as a cultural and spiritual unity, a western counterpart to the Christian empire of Constantinople. And because this unity rested on a common devotion to St Peter, it was natural that the peoples it comprised should look to the pope as its head. This was the great change whose beginnings we can trace back into the early years of the eighth century; it created the foundations on which, three centuries later, a revitalized papacy would rise to new heights.

EMPIRE AND PAPACY

Despite its close attachment to the monarchy, the Frankish church also was affected by the new currents. Already at the time of the great reform synods between 742 and 747 we can perceive a dichotomy which is never again entirely absent and which comes into the full light of day a century later during the pontificate of Nicholas I (858–67). For though it was the king, as we have seen, who initiated the reforms, who presided over the synods and promulgated their decrees as laws of the Frankish state, the spirit behind the reforms was Roman through and through. Pippin might assert control as governor of the church of his land; but the purpose for which his control was used was to bring the Frankish church into conformity with Roman ritual and discipline, to force the clergy to live according to the regulations laid down by the Roman church centuries earlier. Pippin himself, in 746, sent the pope a long list of questions – no less than twenty-seven – on fundamental points of canon law; and in this way, whether he intended it or not, he gave implicit recognition to the pope's authority and position at the head of the church.

No doubt the inherent conflict between the claims of the monarchy and the claims of the papacy was not recognized at the time. But it was there in embryo. And the same ambivalence is apparent under Pippin's son, Charles the Great. Though Charles was far more insistent than his father on his own supremacy, it was nevertheless he who ordered the collection of canons and papal decretals compiled in Rome at the end of the fifth century by Dionysius Exiguus – the first compilation which specifically stressed the pope's legislative authority – to be used officially in the Frankish church. And it is significant that Charles unhesitatingly turned to the pope for authorization when he desired to raise Salzburg to a metropolitan see in 798. This recourse to Rome, which occurred again when new ecclesiastical provinces were founded at Hamburg in 831, at Magdeburg in 968 and at Gniezno in Poland in 1000, is a clear indication of the pope's authoritative position, evidence that there were decisions which no ruler, however exalted, could make alone or even with the support of the clergy of his land. But the most striking instance of the pope's special prerogatives occurred in 799 when Leo III was accused of the crimes of perjury and adultery. The accusation, as we know from Alcuin, caused consternation in ecclesiastical circles. What would happen to the authority of St Peter if his vicar were brought to judgment like an ordinary criminal? In fact, of course, the trial of popes on criminal charges had been frequent enough in the Roman empire; but after long deliberation it was decided to allow Leo to purge himself by oath, in order to preserve the honour of the papacy inviolate. The principle *prima sedes a nemine iudicatur* had been enunciated in similar circumstances by a forger during the pontificate of pope Symmachus at the beginning of the sixth century; but it was paradoxical that it should have been left to Charles the Great, who was so convinced of his superiority to the pope, to make it an established fact. Henceforward it constituted an important element in the papal armoury.

Already, therefore, before Leo III crowned Charles emperor in St Peter's on Christmas Day, 800, there were ambiguities which might easily give rise to conflict. Relations between Charles and Hadrian I at the end of the latter's pontificate had been anything but smooth, and, in the long run, there is no doubt that Charles' acquisition of the imperial title increased

20, 21 Left, tenth-century representation of the clerical hierarchy. Right, the canons of Dionysius which were officially used in the Frankish church; a copy made in the tenth–eleventh century of the collection of canons originally compiled at the end of the fifth century

rather than reduced the underlying tension. The mere fact that the papacy, which for so long had moved in an eastern orbit, was now associated finally and definitely with the new empire in the west had wide implications. There was at least the likelihood that the old conflicts, which had embittered relationships between the popes and the Roman emperors in the past, would be transferred to the western empire, particularly as Charles was determined to surrender none of the powers or prerogatives of his imperial predecessors. The existence of two concurrent powers, both claiming authority over western Christendom, was inherently explosive. No doubt the two powers might, and often did, work in harmony; and this was the ideal. But there was no guarantee that they would; and it was unlikely that the papacy, which Hadrian I, writing to Charles in 790 or 791, had proudly described as 'caput totius mundi', would permanently acquiesce in the position of first bishop of the new western empire, which seemed to be all that Charles was prepared to concede.

It is therefore fair to say that the coronation of Charles as emperor set the stage for the later conflicts of empire and papacy, which were to play so important a part in the evolution of papal claims and doctrines. But these consequences became evident only in the course of the ninth century, and the immediate significance of the events of 800 is more difficult to evaluate. We can only guess the motives which guided Leo III when he crowned Charles emperor; and this is not the place to consider the endless controversies surrounding his actions. The probability, on the whole, is that he had no long-term objectives in mind. Morally and politically discredited, Leo was confronted in 799 by a conspiracy which nearly cost him his life; and we may surmise that his only thought, in investing Charles with imperial powers, was to set up an authority in Rome which could extricate him from his difficulties. But if it would be unwise to credit Leo with grandiose schemes, the situation was clearly one the papacy could turn to profit. If the pope had taken the initiative – and this was an undoubted fact – could it not be argued that the emperor owed his title to the pope? And in that case it was easy to draw the conclusion that the imperial dignity was an office held at the pope's behest, the emperor the secular arm of the church wielding the sword on behalf of the vicar of St Peter. The forged Donation of Constantine supported this theory; for according to this document the first Christian emperor had conferred the imperial insignia on the pope and handed over to him all the provinces of the west.

This was the papal theory of the empire, which was developed to its logical conclusion centuries later by Innocent IV and Boniface VIII. Its theoretical formulation reaches back to Nicholas I (858–67), but it must have been in existence earlier, at least in a rudimentary form, if we are to judge by Charles the Great's actions between 800 and 814. His statement that he would never have entered St Peter's on Christmas Day, 800, if he had been aware of the pope's intention, is well known; and in fact he never returned to Italy thereafter, and kept the pope at arm's length. All his efforts were bent on securing an independent basis for his title by negotiation with Constantinople. When this was achieved in 812, he at once proceeded to secure the succession for his son, and the forms of Louis' coronation in 813 – the fact that it took place in Aachen, not in Rome, and that Charles himself placed the crown on his son's head – can only be interpreted as a direct and intentional rejection of the papal theory of the empire.

The story of the next fifty or sixty years is the story of the breakdown of this attempt to establish an empire independent of Rome and free from papal interference. It is also the story of the emancipation of the papacy from the strict control instituted by Charles the Great and of the assertion of its claim to take the place of the bankrupt empire at the head of western Christendom. Its background was the collapse of the Carolingian empire under the impact of invasion from without – Rome itself was attacked by the Saracens in 846, the two great Roman basilicas, St Peter's and St Paul's, sacked and pillaged – and of dissension and civil war at home.

Even before these disasters occurred, the papacy had begun to re-establish the links between the empire and Rome which had snapped in 812 and 813. In doing so, it played upon the genuine religious convictions of Louis the Pious, and was helped by the death in 816 of the disreputable Leo III, whom Charles to the end had treated with disdain. Leo's successor, Stephen IV (816–17), a man of different mettle, immediately took the initiative, crossed the Alps (like Stephen II in 754), and persuaded Louis to receive benediction at his hands and to be crowned again, this time by the pope himself with a special crown he had brought with him from Rome. The coronation of 816 was a first, tentative move, but it was not decisive; for the very next year Louis had his son made emperor exactly as he himself had been made emperor in 813. But Lothar, crowned at Aachen in 817, allowed himself to be persuaded by Paschal I (817–24) to be crowned again in Rome in 823; and this further step was significant not only because it reaffirmed the connection with the papacy but also because it re-established the link with Rome. And this time, significantly enough, the pope invested the emperor with a sword, the symbol of his obligation to use his office 'ad defensionem ipsius ecclesiæ et imperii'.

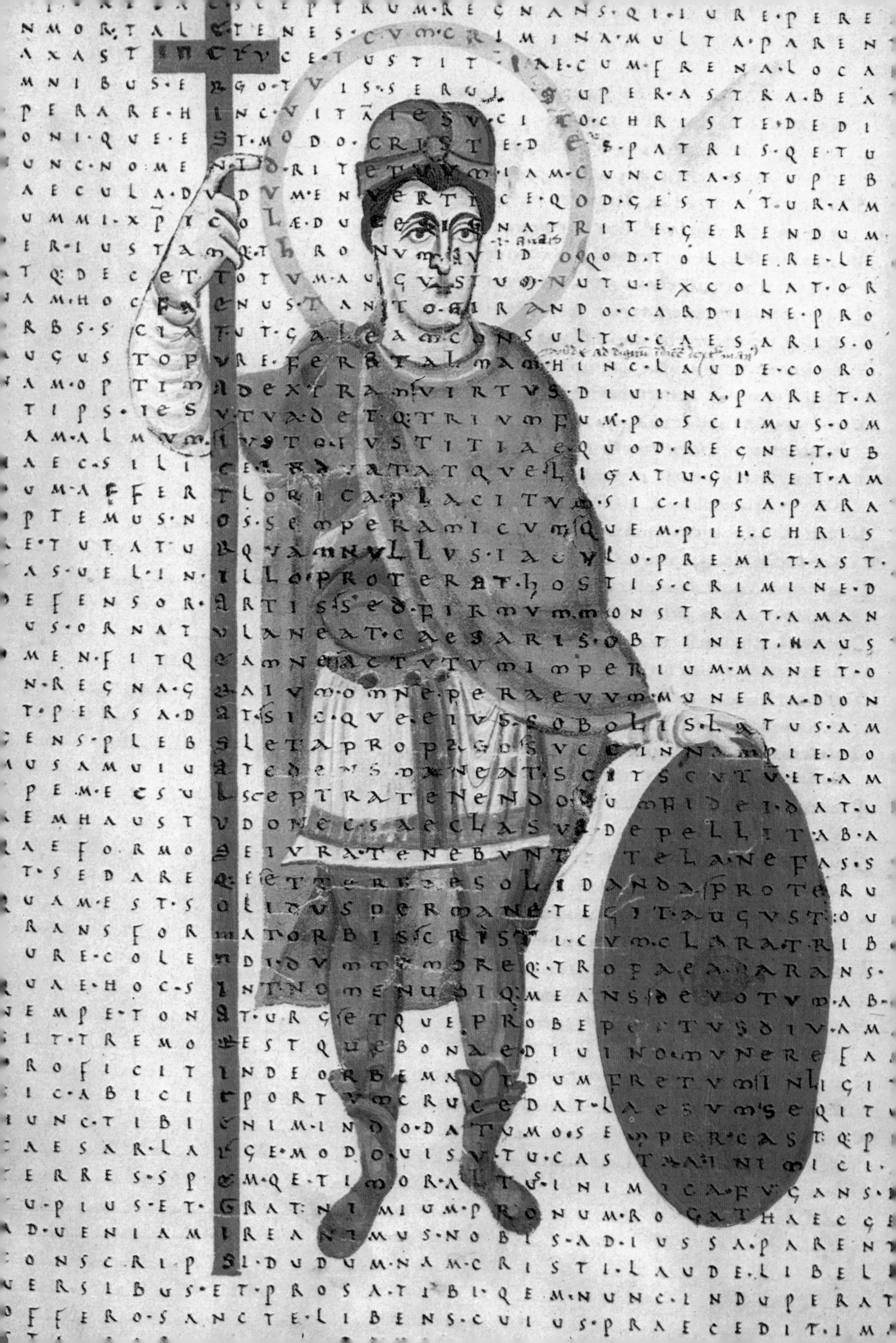

What made these results definitive was the outbreak of civil war in the Frankish lands in 829. The conflicts within the royal dynasty gave the pope his opportunity. In 833 Gregory IV entered the contest on Lothar's side against his father, Louis, opposing his authority as pope, the 'sacra iussio apostolicæ sedis', to the 'sacra iussio imperialis', and boldly asserting the superiority of the 'government of souls, which is the pope's', to the temporal rule of the emperor. As so often, Gregory's intervention misfired, producing a reaction in Louis' favour; but before long there was a strong party which looked to the pope as the only arbiter who could restore peace and unity to the empire.

This situation was aggravated by the conflicts between Louis' sons, after the emperor's death in 840, and the division of the Frankish territories at Verdun in 843. The rival claimants angled for papal support, and sought coronation at the pope's hands to augment their status. In this respect the reign of Lothar's son, Louis II, was a turning-point. Louis was anointed twice (844, 850) and crowned three times (844, 850, 872) by the pope; and through these repeated acts the precedent was established that the pope alone had the right to consecrate the emperor. After 850 there is no further instance of the creation of an emperor except at Rome and by the pope. And when Louis died in 875, it was the pope, John VIII (872–82), who offered the imperial crown to Charles the Bald as a 'beneficium Dei', conferred 'by the privilege of the apostolic see'.

In this way, the popes of the ninth century gradually extricated themselves from the position of subordination in which Charles the Great had placed the papacy. In particular, the pontificate of Nicholas I (858–67) saw a rapid development of the papal theory of the empire. Nothing, perhaps, contributed more to quicken Nicholas' sense of the dignity of the papacy than the revival of the old controversy with Constantinople and the attack on the doctrine of papal primacy by the patriarch Photios and the Byzantine emperor, Michael III. But Nicholas was quick to turn against the emperor of the west the theory of primacy he formulated against the emperor of the east. The purpose for which the empire existed, he told Louis II, was 'the exaltation and peace of his mother, the holy and apostolic church'.

Nicholas staked out no new claims for the papacy; but the firmness with which he asserted his right to intervene against unjust rulers made a lasting impression. He acted, a contemporary wrote, 'as though he were lord of the world', and when he wrote to kings, his letters were 'full of terrible maledictions' such as no previous pope had ever used. He also set the tone for his two immediate successors, Hadrian II (867–72) and John VIII (872–82).

When John VIII insisted on the pope's right, as the divinely ordained head of Christendom, to exercise political supervision over the empire, he was only applying principles asserted by Nicholas I. Nevertheless the importance of John VIII's conception of Christian society as a single body politic under the political and spiritual leadership of the pope is considerable. It marked a decisive stage in the progress of the papacy from spiritual to political primacy, the beginning of its attempt to absorb the state into the church, and the emergence of the hierocratic pretensions which Gregory VII later endeavoured – to the church's lasting detriment – to realize in practice.

The importance of the ninth century in the history of the papacy lay in the precedents it established for the future. It should not, however, be supposed that progress was unchecked. First of all, the claim of the pope to intervene in the empire as the supreme guardian of peace and justice was challenged by the Frankish church, led by archbishop Hincmar of Rheims. Faced by the growing anarchy, Hincmar's remedy was to strengthen the power of the episcopacy, or more particularly of the great metropolitans, and this inevitably led to conflict with Rome. Indeed, we may say without exaggeration that the resistance of the Frankish prelates to the encroachments of Gregory IV and Nicholas I was the beginning of the great struggle, which came to a head under Gregory VII, between the national churches, seeking to retain their traditional autonomy, and the papacy, seeking to reduce them to dependence. The irony of the situation was that the bishops, to maintain their position against the secular power, were forced to rely on the authority of the pope; and so, by a singular paradox, the famous 'Pseudo-Isidorian Decretals', forged in all probability at Rheims about 850 as a means of buttressing episcopal power, became one of the most effective weapons in the papal armoury.

But if the ninth-century papacy had to face the challenge of the Frankish church, it had more immediate problems nearer home. Looked at in an Italian context, its history was decidedly chequered. The unrest in Rome which had punctuated Leo III's unhappy pontificate was the rule, rather than the exception. Paschal I (817–24), accused of complicity in murder, had to clear himself, like Leo, by compurgation; he was so detested in Rome that he could not be buried in St Peter's. After the death of Gregory IV in 844 party conflicts led to a double election which was settled only by imperial intervention, and there was a similar crisis after the death of Leo IV in 855. The truth was that the papacy, having acquired temporal power in Rome and the surrounding territory, was quite incapable of exercising it effectively. In fact, after 824, the administration was brought under imperial supervision through an envoy permanently resident in Rome and papal elections were made dependent on the emperor's ratification. The constitution of 824, which embodied these regulations, showed clearly enough that the emperor had no intention of abdicating his control of the papacy, or leaving the pope a free hand in his Italian territories. Nevertheless, it was accepted with little demur; for the papacy's need of the emperor's support was every bit as great as the emperor's need of the pope's. But precisely here was where the problem lay. So long as Louis II ruled in Italy – that is to say, from 850 to 875 – the system worked reasonably well. But on Louis' death, effective imperial government ceased in Italy, and the pope was left to his own devices, to cope as best he could.

The result was disastrous. Louis's successor, Charles the Bald, the nominee of pope John VIII, failed completely. Harassed by the Normans and by his brother, the king of Germany, he had too much to do in France to spare time for Italy. When Charles died in 877 the pope hurried to France, planning to restore peace and amity among the Carolingian princes, and thus to secure the help he so badly needed. It was a hopeless project. Real power in Italy now lay in the hands of the duke of Spoleto. Against him John tried with little success to mobilize the German Carolingians, Carlman and Charles the Fat. He was also reduced to paying tribute to the Saracens, who had renewed their pressure. And in Rome there was discontent and dissidence. A first conspiracy in 876 was discovered and put down. Six years later John's enemies struck again, and this time successfully. On 15 December 882 John VIII was murdered, the first pope to die at the hands of an assassin.

His successors, Marinus I (882–84) and Hadrian III (884–85), were ephemeral figures. So were most of the succeeding pontiffs. Between 896 and 898 no fewer than six popes followed each other in quick succession. With the total collapse of the Carolingian empire on the death of Charles the Fat in 888, all they could do was to make the best terms possible with the potentates who actually exercised power in Italy. In 891 Guy of Spoleto, having defeated his rival, the marquis of Friuli, in battle, was duly consecrated emperor by pope Stephen V; the following year pope Formosus conferred the same title on Guy's son, Lambert. Naturally the papacy put the best face it could on the situation. Already in 879 John VIII had sternly ordered the Lombard bishops not to recognize anyone as king of Italy without his consent, 'for he whom we are to ordain to the empire ought first to be called and elected by us'. This statement, it has correctly been observed, is the first instance of the claim to approve the election of the future emperor, of which Innocent III (1198–1216) was later to make such devastating use. But the immediate reality was very different. What John VIII was recognizing was the sobering fact that the imperial title was the prize of anyone who could lay hands on the Italian throne. The best the papacy could do to maintain its independence was to try to hold a balance between the contending parties.

But even this availed it nothing. Lambert may have been a phantom emperor, but he insisted on the full exercise of imperial powers, so far as the papacy was concerned. In 898 the constitution promulgated by Lothar in 824 was solemnly re-enacted. The emperor's rights of jurisdiction in Rome were formally recognized, and it was laid down that no pope was to be consecrated except in the presence of the emperor's legates. But this time, instead of a Carolingian ruling the undivided Frankish empire, the emperor was a local Italian potentate, successor of the Lombard dukes who had threatened the papacy in the eighth century. In this respect the wheel had gone full circle; the papacy, as Duchesne remarked, was 'back in the situation of 754'. The importance of the ninth century in the history of the papacy lay, as has already been observed, in the precedents it established for the future. But as a self-contained chapter of papal history it ended in bankruptcy. After 887 the papacy was unable to help itself, still less to exercise the proud claims to the leadership of western Christendom enunciated by Nicholas I. What was needed, as in the days of St Boniface, was a breath of fresh air from north of the Alps; but here also the times were not propitious.

III THE AGE OF REFORM

By the end of the ninth century the fortunes of the papacy were once again at a low ebb. After the final collapse of the Carolingian empire in 887 Italy was left to its own devices, and the papacy, which only a few years earlier, under Nicholas I (858–67), had staked out high claims as the arbiter between contending claimants to the imperial throne, was dragged down into the mire of Italian politics.

Little would be gained by discussing in detail the history of the popes between John VIII (872–82) and John XII (955–64), that 'dissolute boy', eighteen years old when he became holy pontiff, who died, according to the scandal-mongering bishop Liutprand of Cremona, of amorous excess while making love. Few popes in the century following John VIII died peacefully in their beds. As we have seen, John VIII himself was murdered; Stephen VI (896–97) strangled in prison; Benedict VI (973–74) smothered; John XIV (983–84) done to death in the Castel Sant'Angelo. The fact is that they were noblemen appointed for reasons of family policy or politics, scions of the different aristocratic families – the house of Alberic, the Crescentii from the Sabine hills, and later the counts of Tusculum – which were striving to establish themselves as hereditary rulers over the duchy of Rome. But the result was that the papacy, once again, was on the point of losing its moral prestige and its hold over Christendom and becoming simply the instrument of local Italian factions.

Nor was the situation more than temporarily altered when Otto I of Germany intervened in Italy and was crowned emperor by John XII in 962. German rule did something to restore stability; but it was too intermittent and too spasmodic to bring permanent improvement. Otto II strove to break the hold of the Roman factions by bringing in his chancellor, bishop Peter of Pavia, as pope John XIV, but without success. Otto III went further and appointed a German, Gregory V (996–99), and a Frenchman, Gerbert of Aurillac, as pope Sylvester II (999–1003). But the Germans could only control Rome by allying with one Roman faction against another, and the result was that in the first half of the eleventh century the papacy fell under the spell of the counts of Tusculum; indeed, in 1012, the head of the

63

◀ 24 King Henry I of France (1031–60) grants a charter of liberties to the Cluniac abbey of St-Martin-des-Champs; from a contemporary chronicle

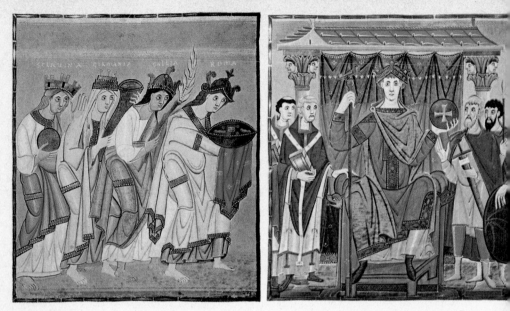

25, 26 The emperor Otto III (right), receiving the homage of the four parts of the empire (left)

Tusculan family had himself made pope as Benedict VIII, and was succeeded in 1024 by his brother, John XIX, and in 1032 by the latter's nephew, Benedict IX. The papacy was evidently on the way to becoming the family possession of the ruling Roman dynasty.

What rescued the papacy from this fate was a reform movement coming from outside. Just as in the eighth century the Anglo-Saxons had restored papal prestige and status in the west, so in the eleventh century movements for the reform of the church springing up in Burgundy and Lorraine gave the papacy a new sense of mission. Since they impinge only indirectly on the story of the popes these reform movements cannot be considered in detail. But they are too important to be taken for granted. In the widest sense, they may be described as the reaction of the church, which suffered most, to the anarchy which resulted from the Viking, Magyar and Saracen invasions of the ninth century, and to ills which secular society had proved itself incapable of remedying. And it was no accident that they sprang up in the lands of the old 'Middle Kingdom', in Burgundy and Lorraine, for it was here that the anarchy was worst, and there was no authority capable of defending the church.

Such conditions were bound to produce a reaction. It was a spontaneous reaction, which originated in the monasteries, because the bishops everywhere were caught up, in the spirit of Carolingian government, in affairs of state. It was a movement which owed everything to the piety of a few great noblemen, who took the initiative in founding new, reformed houses, the lives of whose inmates were intended to be a reproach to those of the monks in the older, secularized foundations. Of the reformed houses the most famous is Cluny, founded in 910 by duke William of Aquitaine in a remote corner of the French duchy of Burgundy, some fifteen miles beyond the border of the Burgundian kingdom. But the role of Cluny should not be exaggerated. It was only one of many centres, equally effective in the revival of monastic life; and it was only later, through its unique organization, that it became outstanding.

Almost contemporary with Cluny – it was founded in 914 – was Brogne in the duchy of Brabant, which became the centre of reform for the entire diocese of Liège. Thence the revival spread southward to Gorze, near Metz, which was reformed in 933, and in the next generation 'Gorzean' reform penetrated slowly up the valley of the Moselle. The ancient abbey of St Maximin at Trier was also affected, and St Maximin carried the movement into the province of Cologne, where old houses were reformed and new reformed houses, such as Gladbach, were founded. In this work Otto I's

27, 28 The famous abbey church of Cluny was destroyed during the French revolution, except for one transept (right) of the abbey church; among the few other remains is the carving (above) representing a 'tone' of plainsong

brother, Bruno, archbishop of Cologne, whom Otto had made 'governor' of Lorraine, played some part; but none of the Ottos paid much attention to reform, and it was only later, in the eleventh century, that it secured royal patronage. Nevertheless the movement soon extended to the upper Rhinelands. Between 929 and 934 the famous abbey of Einsiedeln in Alsace was founded; and from Einsiedeln St Wolfgang carried the reform into Bavaria, founding new monasteries like Tegernsee and Niederaltaich, and reforming the ancient abbey of St Emmeran in Regensburg. Hence the movement spread northwards, via Bamberg. From Niederaltaich St Godehard moved north to Hersfeld in 1005, and after he became bishop of Hildesheim in 1022, he carried reform into the whole of Saxony.

Meanwhile, parallel to this movement of reform stemming from Brogne and originating in Lorraine, Cluny itself was carrying out the reform of centre after centre of monastic life in a widening circle spreading from Burgundy into Aquitaine, thence into Spain, north to Normandy, and south into Italy. The abbey of Fleury-sur-Loire became a centre for expansion to south and west. From St Bénigne at Dijon the Cluniac movement penetrated into Italy, where the abbey of Fruttuaria was founded in 1003; but already as early as 936 the famous abbot of Cluny, Odo, had intervened personally in Rome, and a generation later Cluniac influence was making itself felt in the monastery of San Bonifacio e Sant'Alessio on the Aventine. In Germany, where the Lorraine movement had a firm hold, Cluniac influence was slower to penetrate. Its direct impact was only felt on any scale between 1060 and 1072; but thereafter the Cluniac congregation of Hirsau spread rapidly in the south-west. It was Hirsau that brought the Cluniac spirit to Germany.

The reform movements, of course, had serious opposition to overcome, particularly from the bishops and the older Benedictine houses, which resisted all attempts to change their traditional way of life. In the end, it was only the support of the monarchy which overcame resistance. In France the second king of the Capetian dynasty, Robert the Pious (996–1031), lent his backing to the Cluniacs. In Germany all the kings of the eleventh century, in their different ways, supported the reformers of the Lorraine school. It was through the intervention of Henry II (1002–24) that the ancient abbeys of Fulda, Reichenau, Corvey and Prüm, which had hitherto successfully resisted, were reformed and shorn of their excessive wealth. Henry's successor, Conrad II (1024–39), a man of different mettle, used the church for political purposes; but he also remained on terms of close intimacy with the leader of the reform party in Germany, abbot Poppo of Stablo. Conrad's son, Henry III (1039–56), who married a daughter of the duke of Aquitaine, hereditary patron of Cluny, was the intimate friend of abbot Odilo of Cluny, who watched with sympathy Henry's efforts to reform the church in Germany and Italy and his determination to destroy the ascendancy of the Roman aristocracy over the papacy. Henry III's reign placed the reform movement, particularly in its Cluniac form, in the saddle. Cluny, its abbots the friends and advisers of kings and emperors, was now a major power in Europe.

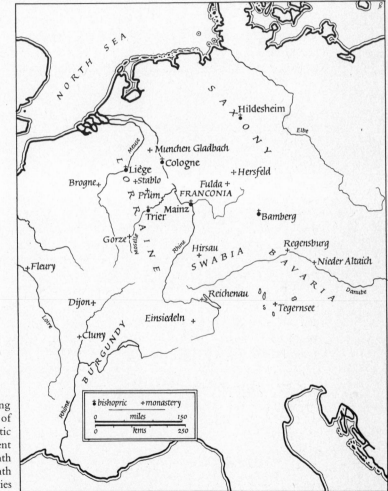

29 Map showing the spread of the monastic reform movement in the tenth and eleventh centuries

30 Overleaf, the consecration of the abbey church of Cluny by pope Urban II in 1095. At left is the pope, and at right St Hugh, under whom the building of this church was begun in 1088. From a late twelfth-century manuscript ▶

phii caudetis faciante alta
ria. Tunc papa ur̄ faciedo miſ
ſaſq̃; agendo. p̄ alia ſalutis hor
tamta. cor̄ epiſ ꝯ cardmalibuſ
multoꝝq̃; p̄ſomſ. huiceṁodi
ſerſem habuit ad p̄plm.

omanu ſcilicet pontificio
e numero uel ordini diuina
ignatio licet indignum aſ
uit: me olim monachum
enq; monaſterii huius. ſub
no ac uenerabili hugone

31 Easter service at the Benedictine monastery of Monte Cassino; miniature from an eleventh-century manuscript

There was thus no fundamental conflict between the aims of the monastic reformers and those of the monarchy. The king, with his sense of divine ministry, was the most likely ally of the reformers in their attempt to free the churches from the heavy hand of the lay aristocracy; and the reformers for the most part accepted the king's rights over the church, which were hallowed by long usage and recognized in the collections of canon laws in use in the first half of the eleventh century. Cluny itself, for example, re-formed royal abbeys in France like St Maur and St Denis, but did not think of demanding that the king, in exchange, should surrender the smallest fraction of his rights over them. But as reform went deeper, the first glimmerings of doubt began to appear. Already at the close of the tenth century, the famous abbot of Fleury, Abbo, was starting to have suspicions. 'Let him,' he wrote, 'who wishes the health of his soul, beware of believing that the church belongs to any save God alone. For He said to Peter, the Prince of the Apostles: "I will give thee My church"; "Mine", not "thine" ... In truth, dear princes, we neither live nor speak as Catholics when I say "this church is mine", and some other says "that church is his".'

Similar ideas were expressed at the same period, or slightly later, in the other centre of reform, in Lorraine. Siegfried of Gorze, Gerard of Cambrai and Wazo of Liège asserted that the only law recognizable in the church was that of the canons; and their attitude shows a first inkling of discrepancy between the ancient canon law and eleventh-century practice. Meanwhile, in Italy, in or around 1031, Guido of Arezzo began to agitate against what he called the 'simony' of the German kings, and branded lay investiture of bishops as heresy. The centre of agitation was Milan, where social unrest merged with the movement for reform in the church; but the movement soon spread to other parts of Lombardy in spite of the opposition of the bishops and the German government. As yet, however, Rome was scarcely affected. The Tusculan popes of the early eleventh century were probably not as hostile or indifferent to reform as used to be thought. But they were tied down, as we have seen, in the tradition of an aristocratic, dynastic papacy; and the effort to maintain their position in Rome against rival aristocratic factions – which seemed impossible unless they could build up a strong territorial foundation – absorbed all their energies. On the whole, this policy brought about a revival of the papacy from the depths to which it had sunk in the tenth century. But it still remained immersed in local Roman connections, its field of vision narrowly Italian. The breath of fresh air from north of the Alps had scarcely reached it.

It was only when this narrow localism had been overcome that the papacy was in a position to play an active part in the reform movement. This was the work of the emperor Henry III. At the end of 1044 an opposition party in Rome drove out the last Tusculan pope, Benedict IX, and raised in his place a member of the rival aristocratic faction, Sylvester III. But Sylvester was hard put to it to maintain his position against Benedict, while the latter seems to have realized that his own position was in the long run untenable. Hence Benedict abdicated, on payment of a considerable pension, and his place was taken by a new pope, Gregory VI, a man of high moral standing and reforming spirit.

At this stage Henry III intervened. At a synod held at Sutri in 1046 Gregory VI was deposed on the grounds of simony, i.e., that the sums paid to Benedict IX amounted to buying the holy see – a view about which modern historians have argued, but which certainly was shared by contemporary reformers, including abbot Odilo of Cluny. Then, for further caution, Sylvester and Benedict were also deposed, although the former appears to have abandoned his claims in 1045 and the latter had certainly abdicated. But Henry evidently wanted to make a clean sweep. Whether his reasons

ontigit ut nonuſ Leo benediceret Almuſ

DOMN
PAPA
LEO·HOR·

Domn abbas
VVALARiuſ

were political or religious hardly matters. Henry's purpose was 'to lift the papacy out of the field of Roman party politics'; and this was as desirable for political as for moral or religious reasons. It was because the papacy was the prize of Roman party factions that schism and simony had occurred; and the popes chosen in this way had not only scarcely ever been selected because of their suitability for their spiritual tasks, but had also been politically unreliable. This state of affairs Henry determined in 1046 to end. Hence, having deposed the nominees of the Roman factions, he immediately had himself made *patricius*, a title which, according to the ideas prevalent in Rome at the time, conferred the right to control the election of the pope.

Henry III's use of his new powers was characteristic. In quick succession four German bishops were raised to the papacy: Clement II (1046–47), Damasus II (1048), Leo IX (1049–54) and Victor II (1055–57). All were ardent reformers, and undoubtedly chosen as such; but three of the four died too soon to leave a decisive mark, and of the four pontificates it is that of Leo IX, an Alsatian nobleman, near relative of the emperor himself, who had previously been bishop of Toul, that stands out.

32 Pope Leo IX, whose reforms laid the foundation of the papal monarchy, is shown here with Warinus, abbot of St Arnulf of Metz

33 Henry III, the emperor who emancipated the papacy from the control of Roman factions and introduced the spirit of reform to Rome; this contemporary portrait shows him standing between two bishops

73

Leo IX has been described as 'the real founder of the papal monarchy over the church'. He brought with him to Rome the leaders of the reform movement in the north, particularly Humbert of Moyenmoutier, whom he made cardinal-bishop of Silva Candida in 1050, and so surrounded himself by advisers and helpers who were remote from the Roman aristocracy. The chief exception was a certain Hildebrand, a Roman clerk, who had been Gregory VI's chaplain, and who had gone with him after 1046 into exile in Germany. Hildebrand, because of his acquaintance with local Roman conditions, was put in charge of the papal estates, to safeguard them from aristocratic depredation and to restore the material resources of the papacy, which had suffered in the party contests of the previous generation; but he was still a lesser figure, merely a subdeacon, and the lead from 1049 definitely passed to the reformers from Lorraine.

Thus it was the spirit of reform as it had grown in Lorraine, rather than that of Cluny, that began, with Leo IX, to transform the papacy. Precisely because they were strangers to Rome, the new men brought with them new ideas of the pope's functions and dignity. The Italian popes had been bound up in Italian territorial questions and in the maintenance of their position among the contending Roman factions. Outside Italy they had intervened fitfully and infrequently, occasionally defining points of doctrine or deciding legal disputes between churchmen; but they had no conception of themselves as leaders of Christendom – even of western Christendom – and little notion of the papacy as a universal power. This only came with the northern influx. The idea of the papacy as a moral force, or as the directing head of a Christian community, took shape north of the Alps, first in the hands of the Anglo-Saxon missionaries in the days of St Boniface, and then in the hands of the eleventh-century reformers. They had more belief in the papacy than the popes themselves, and above all they had a clear idea of the reforming purposes to which papal authority should be put.

It was this new concept of the papacy and its place in the church that accounted for the immense and unprecedented activity which began as soon as Leo IX became pope. From the start Leo refused to be bogged down in Roman politics. He left Rome in May 1049, barely three months after his consecration, and during his pontificate of over five years spent hardly more than six months in the city. He crossed the Alps three times to France and Germany, where he held synod after synod, issuing decrees against simony, clerical marriage, violence and moral laxity, and where he settled countless disputes.

In this way papal authority became real and visible. The practical result was that the papacy, hitherto an object of shame and scandal to serious churchmen, won the support of the reforming movement. It won the backing of Cluny, and that meant that for the first time an effective force, the closely-knit Cluniac congregation with all its international ramifications, was at the pope's disposal within the church. But contact with Rome had a second result, scarcely less significant than the first. It changed, not without heart-searching and opposition from within the reforming ranks, the direction and character of the reform movement. The monastic reformers of Lorraine and Burgundy, and their disciples in France and Germany and England, had thought primarily of raising the standard of clerical and secular life by precept and example; they sought moral reform within the framework of the existing law and constitution of the church. Contact with the papacy brought a change. When the spirit of reform penetrated to Rome, and came into contact with an Italian and Mediterranean environment, it was imperceptibly altered. For the Romans who joined the reformers the first consideration was not moral rejuvenation, but the reinforcement of papal authority.

This quickly became clear in two directions. The one was relations with Constantinople, the other was the evolution of canon law. During the Tusculan period the Greek and Roman churches, which had been at loggerheads in the days of Nicholas I, had reached a *modus vivendi*, each co-existing relatively peacefully in its own sphere; but the new conceptions of papal authority the reformers brought with them to Rome after the accession of Leo IX undermined this compromise. When in 1054 the pope dispatched a delegation headed by cardinal Humbert to Constantinople, the claims to universal authority it put forward on behalf of the papacy, and the equally intransigent reaction of the patriarch Kerullarios, quickly brought about an open breach between the two churches. The controversy between Humbert and Kerullarios resulted in the formulation of the exalted claims which Gregory VII later turned against the emperor Henry IV; translated from the spiritual to the political sphere, they were to become the platform for the papal attack on the empire. Meanwhile, the law of the church was being reshaped on parallel lines. Down to the middle of the eleventh century, the current canon law had been that set out in the *Decretum* compiled about 1012 by bishop Burchard of Worms. But about 1050 a great new collection of canons, the so-called 'Collection in 74 titles', made its appearance. It was the first book of canon law to be put together in Rome; and characteristically it breathes a new spirit. Burchard, faithfully reflecting the outlook of his age, made scant reference to the pope. He was in no sense anti-papal – he was in close touch with the reforming movement north of the Alps and had studied in the reformed law-schools of Lorraine – but his work reflected the minor role played by the papacy in church affairs in his day. He was concerned above all with questions of clerical morals: the celibacy of the clergy, the traffic in ecclesiastical offices, simony, and moral questions such as the indissolubility of marriage. The new 'Collection in 74 titles' was very different. Not moral reform, but the assertion of the legal position and prerogatives of the successor of Peter, was its primary concern; and it drew for its authority on papal letters, or decretals, rather than on the Fathers or on synodal decrees.

The contrast between the *Decretum* of Burchard of Worms and the 'Collection in 74 titles' shows the way things were moving. Nevertheless it should not be exaggerated. For all its emphasis on the rights of the papacy, the new law-book made no attack on the rights of the laity, or more specifically on the position of the king in the church. Henry III's intervention in 1046 was regarded as abnormal, justified only by the abnormal circumstances; but down to the emperor's death in 1056 there is little, if any, sign of opposition between the monarchy and the reforming party. It was after 1056, when the reforming movement linked up with forces opposed to the empire, that the decisive change came. How far the breach was deliberate, how far the outcome of a chain of fortuitous events, is debatable. On the whole, the element of deliberate antagonism should not be exaggerated. One person alone among the reformers at the papal court appears to have been opposed on principle to Henry III's position in regard to the papacy; and that was Hildebrand. But Hildebrand was not yet in the front rank. He was passed over by Leo IX in his promotions of cardinals; and although his importance began to grow immediately after Henry III's death in 1056, and in 1057 he was for the first time given an important mission, it was not until the pontificate of Alexander II (1061–73), after the death of the leading figure of the first generation, Humbert of Moyenmoutier (d. 1061), that he began to play the part of 'first minister'. By then the decisive developments had taken place.

Henry III's death, leaving only a child as heir, inevitably made a difference. It was only ten years since, at Sutri, he had introduced the reforming popes. The Tusculan party still remained in existence, and could count on the backing of considerable elements in Rome which, for national reasons, hoped to seize the opportunity provided by the weakening of the German monarchy to free themselves from German domination. For the reformers, for whom it was intolerable that the papacy should again become dependent upon party struggles in Rome, these were important facts; and many things which, viewed in the light of later events, seem to have been directed towards liberating the papacy from imperial control, were really directed towards freeing it – or maintaining its freedom – from Roman factions. But if the German government, under the weak regency of Henry III's widow, Agnes, was no longer able to give them the support they had received from Henry, inevitably the reformers looked elsewhere. In doing so, they came into touch with avowed enemies of the imperial government, whose position Henry III's death had strengthened, and in German eyes they seemed to be deliberately throwing off the control Henry III had exercised.

In this way the position deteriorated. By the time Henry IV took personal command in 1065 – by which time Hildebrand, the future Gregory VII, was already the leading figure at the papal court – the balance had definitely changed. Henry could not be expected to accept conditions during his minority as normal; he was bound to try to restore the position as it was at the time of his father's death. The papacy, on the other hand, which had won new confidence by its success in steering through the perils of the years after 1056, was not prepared to go back to the situation in Henry III's day. Thus, less through deliberate antagonism than through the development of events after 1056, a head-on collision was in preparation. No party wanted it, and it was postponed until after Hildebrand became pope as Gregory VII in 1073. Its causes were political rather than religious. None of the leading reformers, not even cardinal Humbert, intended a direct attack on the monarchy; and a powerful wing, led by St Peter Damiani, wholeheartedly defended the place of the monarchy in the church, believing that only with its active co-operation could simony and the moral corruption of the clergy be extirpated. If conflict was inevitable, it was not as a direct result of the theories enunciated by the reformers, but through the fact that the movement became involved in political events, and perhaps in the final analysis because of the clumsy handling of the political situation by the German government.

GREGORY VII AND THE INVESTITURE CONTEST

The tangled but momentous events between Henry III's death in 1056 and the accession of Gregory VII in 1073 can be summarized only briefly. The first need of the reform party, as already indicated, was for support, and this they obtained from duke Godfrey of Lorraine, who had married the widowed countess of Tuscany in 1054 and was the most powerful person in central Italy. Godfrey was the 'stormy petrel' of the eleventh century. He had been at loggerheads with Henry III since 1044; and when on the death in 1057 of the last of the popes nominated by Henry, the cardinals elected Godfrey's brother as pope Stephen IX, and on Stephen's sudden death in the following year they chose with Godfrey's assent the bishop of Florence (Florence being the centre of Godfrey's Tuscan lands), it was a momentous decision. In this way links were formed between the reform movement and the elements of feudal opposition in Germany and Italy, and the reformers became suspect to the imperial government. Furthermore, the alliance with Godfrey of Lorraine set a precedent; it was the first of a series of alliances which, when consolidated, gave the papacy the material backing through which it could hold its own against any power.

The next step came after the death of Stephen IX in 1058. Before the reformers could act, the Roman party grasped its opportunity, raised the last of the Tusculan popes, Benedict X (1058–59), to the holy see, and took control of Rome. The reformers, driven out to Siena, elected Nicholas II (1059–61), a Burgundian who had become bishop of Florence; but the result was schism. The resultant crisis provoked active measures of fundamental importance, which make Nicholas II's short pontificate unusually significant. First of all, the anti-Norman policy of Leo IX and Stephen IX was reversed. In 1059 Nicholas came to terms with the Normans, granting them Capua, Apulia, Calabria and even Sicily (which still remained to be conquered), as fees held of the papacy in return for an annual payment and military help. It was land which the pope had no legal title to give; and his action was bound to provoke the hostility of both the eastern and the western empires. But it gave the papacy the support of the toughest fighters in contemporary Europe, and Nicholas immediately used it to gain entry to Rome and beat down his opponent, Benedict X. Nor was this Nicholas II's only effort to secure new allies. It was under him that the papacy made contact with the dissident elements in Milan, the so-called Patarini, and with their help forced the archbishop to swear an oath of obedience to the pope, and to receive a second time from his hands the office he had previously received from the emperor. Here again the papacy came into conflict with the imperial government; but by extending its contacts into Lombardy, it now had allies in every part of Italy. At the same time Nicholas set about establishing good relations with France; so much so that it has been said that 'the French alliance completed the alliance with the Normans' of Sicily. From 1060, when a rupture with the German government became imminent, the pope knew that 'in one degree or another he could count on France'.

The other important measure of Nicholas II's pontificate was the famous electoral decree of 1059. This, without doubt, was a response to the double election of 1058; in other words, its object was to prevent a revival of the power of the Roman aristocracy. For the future, the choice of candidates was to be the prerogative of the cardinal-bishops, selection from among them the task of the cardinals as a body; and the rights of the clergy and people of Rome were reduced to formal assent after the election had been otherwise completed. In this way the influence of the Roman aristocracy over papal elections was broken. But regulations of this sort, whether deliberately or not, inevitably affected the emperor's position also. It is true that imperial rights were expressly reserved; but equally clearly, if the cardinals carried out their allotted part, they would be far more limited than those which Henry III had exercised. The emperor would still have a veto, and no one would be pope without his assent; but the actual choice, or nomination, would no longer be his. Furthermore, his participation was treated as a concession by the pope, not as an inherent right of the emperor. Nevertheless, the electoral decree brought no immediate hostile reaction from the imperial government. It was only when, a few months later, the Normans were brought into the picture that trouble arose, for the Normans were regarded by the empire as its deadliest enemy. As part of the agreement with the Normans, Robert Guiscard swore that he would lend his support to any pope chosen by the cardinals. Thus he became guarantor of the new electoral system. This was the last straw for the German government which, at a synod summoned in 1060, condemned Nicholas and annulled all his acts.

Not surprisingly, therefore, Nicholas II's death in 1061 was followed by another schism, this time between the reformers who, with Norman help, elected bishop Anselm of Lucca as Alexander II (1061–73), and the combined forces of the German regency government, the Roman aristocracy and the conservative Lombard bishops, who raised up bishop Cadalus of Parma as pope Honorius II (1061–72). It was a serious blunder on the German side. The empire, which had launched the reform of the papacy, had fundamentally nothing in common with the enemies of reform, whose days, it was already evident, were numbered; and from the start its attitude was uneasy and half-hearted. Even the German archbishops and bishops – although alarmed by papal attempts, in contravention of current practice, to reduce them to a position of subordination – soon wavered and ranged themselves on Alexander's side in 1064; but Cadalus had real support in Lombardy and held out until his death in 1071.

Nevertheless the schism brought a new bitterness into relations, which rapidly deteriorated, and did irreparable damage. This was the first time in history that the emperor, having opted for a candidate, failed to get him accepted; and the blow to imperial prestige was great. Not unnaturally, also, since Henry IV was supporting the anti-pope, the papal party forgot the concessions made to the crown in the electoral decree of 1059. During the ten years' schism between 1061 and 1071 the emphasis changed step by step from moral regeneration of the clergy to the destruction of the rights of the laity, and particularly of the monarchy, which seemed, in fomenting schism, to be the root of the trouble. When the bishop of Florence requested royal approval of his election in the traditional manner, Alexander II issued a stern rebuke. 'Since no emperor or king is permitted to meddle in the church's affairs,' he wrote, 'it is plain that you did this out of contempt for the holy see.' It was not plain at all; but the contrast with the days of Henry III is complete, and so also the contrast with the attitude of the earlier generation of reformers. But by now a new man, Hildebrand, was in the saddle; and with him a new attitude, both to the place of the church in society and to the place of the pope in the church.

Thus we reach the pontificate of Hildebrand himself, elected tumultuously and contrary to the stipulations of the decree of 1059, the very day after Alexander II's death in 1073, with the evident intention of forestalling imperial action. The pontificate of Gregory VII (1073–85) is, by general assent, a turning-point in the history of the medieval papacy; and from the beginning it was clear that things had changed. There was no longer any question of obtaining imperial assent; Gregory merely informed the emperor – just as he informed other kings and princes, bishops and abbots – of his election.

Even so, there was no immediate breach. Perhaps both parties were temporizing. Gregory was having trouble with his Norman allies, with the hostile Lombard bishops and with the Romans; Henry IV was faced, in 1073, with a serious rebellion in Saxony. But on the whole it would be truer to say that the attempts between 1073 and 1075 to find a compromise were genuine. Gregory at this time was planning a great military expedition against the Seljuk Turks who had inflicted a resounding defeat on the eastern empire at Manzikert in 1071 and were overrunning the Holy Land; and for this project agreement and co-operation with Henry IV were necessary. Negotiations between Gregory and Henry continued through the summer and autumn of 1075, and the pope's attitude was accommodating.

Henric̄ quartuſ hen
rici impe ratoriſ filiuſ
admodū puer patri ſuc
cedenſ regnare c̄ępit
bxxxviī loco ab au
guſto & regnauit
annis·L·

34 The emperor Henry IV,
whose clash with Gregory VII
led to a conflict between
empire and papacy which
lasted half a century and was only
concluded by the concordat of
Worms in 1122

But if Gregory's first actions as pope 'reveal', in Fliche's words, 'his invincible desire to unite the two powers, spiritual and temporal, for the reform of the church', the work of reform continued and gathered force. In March 1074 a Roman synod ordered the deposition of all simoniacal priests. In December of the same year all married priests were forbidden to celebrate Mass. These decrees provoked hostile reactions in England, France and Germany; but they were renewed in 1075, and in February of the same year a new Roman synod promulgated the famous decree against lay investiture: 'if anyone in future receives a bishopric or abbey from the hands of any layman, he is under no circumstances to be ranked among the bishops, and we exclude him from the grace of St Peter. . . . And if any emperor, king, prince or any lay power presumes to invest anyone with a bishopric or any ecclesiastical office, let him know that he will therewith incur the sentence of excommunication.'

Even now, however, the issue was postponed. The decree of February 1075 was not immediately enforced, and in July the pope wrote Henry IV a letter which did not mention it. Gregory was still concerned above all with the two issues of simony and clerical morals, and with this in view was still ready to compromise with the lay power. The touchstone was whether kings and princes would co-operate actively in the work of reform, and the decree prohibiting lay investitures was held in hand as a weapon against kings who hindered the papacy in this work; it was a last resort, not an end in itself, but a means to an end. In this sense it may fairly be said that responsibility for the conflict which followed a few weeks later rests on Henry IV. In his attitude to the church Henry IV was certainly a very different man from his father, Henry III. That is not to say that he was opposed to the reform movement. But agreement with Gregory would have meant recognizing the pope's point of view, and it is comprehensible that he thought the price too high. Gregory's attitude on clerical reform had already driven the German bishops, who had refused to support their government against Alexander II, into opposition. There were good reasons to doubt whether the pope's interference in the internal affairs of other metropolitans was warranted by canon law, as understood at the time. Moreover, the pope's support of dissident elements in Lombardy was undermining the position of the German monarchy in northern Italy, which depended on the power of the bishops. Whatever Henry's attitude to reform in principle, Gregory's application of it was not such as to conciliate the emperor. Thus behind the struggle which ensued was a conflict of personalities. Gregory did not trust Henry to carry through the work of reform; Henry did not trust Gregory's professions of conciliation. But behind the personal and political issues was a deeper issue still: the place of the monarchy in Christian society. Henry took up arms in defence of the monarchy, its rights and prerogatives: that, not the secondary question of 'investitures', was the crucial point at issue between 1076 and 1122.

This is not the place to discuss the great conflict of empire and papacy which broke out at the end of 1075. Characteristically it came to a head over the great metropolitan church of Milan, the see of St Ambrose, which regarded itself as in most respects the equal of the bishopric of Rome. In a letter of December 1075 Gregory accused Henry of disobeying the apostolic law in regard to Milan and other sees; then, after insisting that he had been prepared to discuss with Henry the application of the decree against investitures, he broadened his argument, charged Henry with want of respect to 'the prince of the church, that is to say, Peter, the prince of the Apostles', claimed that disobedience to the pope was disobedience to God's will, and in a verbal message reproached him for his evil life, and threatened him not only with excommunication but also with deposition. Henry immediately took up the challenge. In January 1076 a synod was called at Worms. The German and Italian bishops withdrew their obedience; and in a famous letter addressed to 'Hildebrand, no longer pope, but false monk', damned by the judgment of the assembled episcopacy, Henry called upon Gregory to descend from the throne of Peter.

Henry's attitude was bold, but foolish. His violent attack on Gregory turned sympathy over to the side of his opponent. Not only did he misjudge the strength of the reforming currents, but he also underestimated the strength of the forces, both in Germany and in Italy, which were ready to back the pope against him. The sphere of influence, and therewith the resources, of the papacy were far more extensive than at the time of Henry III's death in 1056. The action of the papacy from the pontificate of Leo IX, the growing use of papal legates to infuse a new spirit into the national churches, had already had a marked effect; everywhere, even in Germany, the custom of appealing to the pope from the lower ecclesiastical courts was growing, and the prelates were compelled to submit to papal decisions. Many of the forces which supported Gregory – not least of all, the German princes – may have been self-interested; but they provided the pope with powerful allies. In any event, it was characteristic of Gregory that he did not hesitate to accept Henry's challenge. At the Lenten synod of 1076 in Rome he replied by excommunicating Henry and suspending him from government. Thereafter links were quickly forged between the papacy and the German opposition, and in October 1076 the German princes, at the diet of Tribur, imposed drastic terms on Henry: he was to free himself from excommunication within four months, or else to lose his crown.

The subsequent course of events – Henry's flight in midwinter across the Alps, his famous meeting with the pope at Canossa (January 1077), the breach between the German opposition and Gregory, and the election of Rudolf of Swabia as anti-king (13 March 1077) – is well known. For three years, from 1077 to 1080, Gregory refused to recognize Rudolf, calling instead upon both parties to accept his mediation. When, in 1080, finally despairing of agreement with Henry, Gregory came out on the side of the anti-king, he aroused opposition by declaring that the new ruler was a vassal of the holy see. Even Rudolf, for all his weakness, rejected this claim out of hand. In Germany it alienated public opinion, and the pope's renewal of the excommunication of Henry was regarded as an act of persecution. In reply, Henry raised up an anti-pope, the active, genuinely reformatory Clement III (1080–1100). Gregory's position in Italy crumbled; he was forced, as a last resort, to buy back the alliance of the Normans, with whom he had quarrelled; and having lost Rome to Henry, he died an exile – and virtually a prisoner – in Norman hands at Salerno, in 1085.

The pontificate of Gregory VII is conventionally regarded as the culmination of the reform movement which reached Rome with Leo IX, and Hildebrand himself as the practical exponent of the reform programme theoretically formulated by Humbert of Moyenmoutier in the dark days after the death of pope Stephen IX in 1058, when the Roman reaction and the elevation of the Tusculan Benedict X looked as though it would bring the whole work of reform inaugurated in 1046 crashing down. It was then that Humbert perceived, with sudden force and clarity, that something more than moral regeneration was necessary, and, in the third book of his treatise *Contra simoniacos*, launched a frontal attack on the whole position of laymen and kings within the church.

35 Henry IV with the anti-pope, Guibert of Ravenna (Clement III), and the expulsion of Gregory VII, who dies in exile at Salerno; drawings from a twelfth-century German chronicle

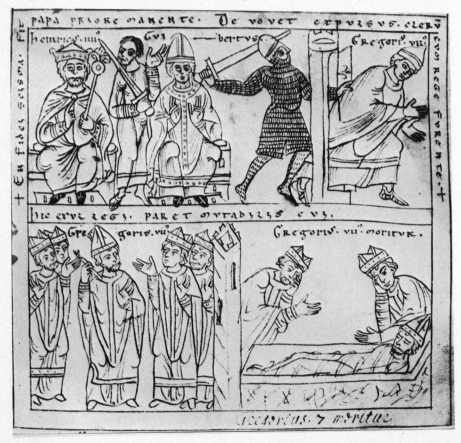

Tempting as it is to regard Humbert as the theoretician of reform and Hildebrand as the executor of Humbert's ideas, this view nevertheless fails to define Gregory VII's place in the reform movement. As Fliche has said, one will look in vain in the works of Peter Damian or cardinal Humbert, or even in the 'Collection in 74 titles', for anything to parallel Gregory's views and actions; and Caspar has pointed out that he departed far from the Cluniac spirit because he was too active to accept the contemplative, ascetic element in the monastic ideal. It is no accident that the abbots of Cluny at no time in the whole course of the struggle between Gregory VII and Henry IV stood wholeheartedly in the papal camp. Both Humbert and Peter Damian had been scholars and theologians of the first rank; Gregory – whom Damian succinctly described as a 'holy Satan' – was a practical man, impatient of argument. His letters – with the sole exception of the two famous letters to Hermann of Metz, defending his power to depose kings – are curt, often illogical, devoid of canonistic learning. He was a man who (as he said on his death-bed) loved and hated passionately, and he was not interested to convince his opponents by logical argument. That there might be truth on the side of his critics scarcely entered his mind; opposition, for him, was due either to stupidity or to criminal folly. He assumed through-out – and this was what alienated contemporary opinion – the identity of his own commands with those of God; hence his inflexibility, hence also, in the guise of a return to the old order, the revolutionary nature of his claims. He was, as Caspar has said, 'in spite of all precursors, the great originator, who stood absolutely by himself'.

We are fortunate in having a key to Gregory's thought and attitude in the famous *Dictatus Papae*, which was entered up in the papal register in the spring of 1075. It is composed of twenty-seven lapidary sentences, entirely personal and evidently never intended for publication; without much doubt, they represent the principles upon which Gregory intended to act and for which he expected his assistants to find justification in biblical, patristic and canonistic authorities. It is here that we see how novel and revolutionary Gregory's attitude was. He claimed to be enforcing the old law of the church, but few of his axioms are supported by the authority of the canons. The second proposition, that the pope alone may be called 'universal', was flatly contradicted by them. The most famous of all (no. 12), that he was empowered to depose emperors, was equally without founda-tion, and arose – as contemporary critics were quick to point out – from a total misunderstanding of a letter of Gregory the Great. But even when he remained within tradition, Gregory VII interpreted it in such a way that it had a new sense. Thus, from the dogma of the pope's succession to St Peter, he deduced that the pope's authority is the authority of Christ. Precisely this deduction both Humbert and Damian had scrupulously avoided drawing; for them 'the fulness of grace remained with Christ himself', and he distributed his gifts not to the pope alone, but to many. This subtle distinction Gregory overlooked, because he was not interested in the finer points of theology, but in the practical results; namely, the enhancement of papal authority. His treatment of the old command that every Catholic church must be in harmony with Rome, was similar; what had been meant was harmony of belief, but Gregory extended it to include liturgy and organization. In the same way, where earlier Roman doctrine had merely insisted that bishops could only be deposed with the consent of the pope, Gregory laid down that the pope or his legates could depose bishops without the co-operation of a synod, and even without the accused being given a hearing.

Doctrines such as these fell like a bomb-shell on the traditional thought of the age. They were poles apart from the aims and endeavours of the earlier reformers. For Gregory, reform was not a matter of preaching and example, but of organization. His object was not to win over souls so much as to reorganize the church and Christian society in such a way as to make it possible to enforce the truth, as it had been revealed to him. To secure the 'liberty' of the church, the church itself and society had to be reorganized on monarchical lines, ecclesiastical administration streamlined in the direction of centralized control, kings and rulers reduced, like the bishops, to the position of executors of the pope's will. The novelty of all this does not appear to have struck Gregory, nor the deeper question – which St Peter Damian had perceived – whether reform, which could only be real when it was the expression of personal conviction, could be obtained in this way. In fact, the struggle which developed in Germany and in Italy after 1076 soon lost all semblance of a reformatory movement. Everywhere monasteries and bishoprics were despoiled, and far from leading to improvement the civil war made bad worse.

The best-known aspect of Gregory's programme was his attack on the kingship. For him the king was a removable official. He had still a divine duty on earth; but he only remained king so long as he performed this duty. If he ceased to act righteously, he became *ipso facto* a tyrant, to whom no duty was owed. And it was for the pope, as successor of Peter and vicar of Christ, to determine when a ruler was acting as *rex iustus*, when he was a tyrant who must be deposed. Thus Gregory turned his back on the ancient

I Q̇d Romana eccla a solo dño sit fundata.

II Q̇d solus Romanus pontifex iure dicat̃ universalis.

III Q̇d ille solus possit deponere epos ul reciliare.

IIII Q̇d legatus eius omnib; epis p̃sit ĩ cõcilio ctã inferioris gradus.
et adversus eos sentẽtia depositiõis possit dare.

V Q̇d absentes papa possit deponere.

VI Q̇d cũ excõmunicatis abillo int̃ cetã nec ĩ eade͂ domo debem̃ manere.

VII Q̇d illi soli licet p̃ temporis necessitate novas leges condere.
novas plebes congregare. de canonica abbatiã facere. et e cõn
tra. divite epm divide. et inopes unire.

VIII Q̇d solus possit uti imprialib; insigniis.

VIIII Q̇d solius papæ pedes õis principes de osculent̃.

X Q̇d illius solius nomẽ ĩ ecclus recitet̃.

XI Q̇d hoc unicũ e nomĩ ĩ mundo.

XII Q̇d illi liceat impatores deponere.

XIII Q̇d illi liceat de sede ad sede necessitate cogente epos transmutare.

XIIII Q̇d de õni eccla quocunq̃ voluerit clericũ valeat ordinare.

XV Q̇d abillo ordinatus alii eccle pee possit. sed n̄ militare. et qd
ab aliquo epo n̄ debet superiore gradũ accipe.

XVI Q̇d nulla synodus absq̃ pcepto eius debet generalis vocari.

XVII Q̇d nullũ capitulũ nullusq̃ liber canonicus habeat̃ absq̃ illius
auctoritate.

XVIII Q̇d sententia illius a nullo debeat retractari. et ipse omium
solus retractare possit.

XVIIII Q̇d a nemine ipse iudicari debeat.

XX Q̇d nullus audeat condēnare aptica sede appellante.

XXI Q̇d maiores causæ cuiuscunq̃ eccle ad eã referri debeant.

XXII Q̇d Romana eccla nunquã erravit nec i̇mppetuũ scriptura
testante errabit.

XXIII Q̇d romanus pontifex si canonice fuerit ordinat meritis b̃i petri in
dubitanter efficit scs. testante sco Ennodio papiensi epo ei mul
tis scis patribus fauentib; sic in decretis beati Symachi ppe cõtinet.

XXIIII Q̇d illius pcepto et licentia subiectis liceat accusare.

XXV Q̇d absq̃ synodali cõventu possit epos deponere et reciliare.

XXVI Q̇d catholicus n̄ habeat̃ qi n̄ cõcordat Romanæ eccle.

XXVII Q̇d a fidelitate iniquorũ subiectos potest absolvere.

36 The *Dictatus Papae* of Gregory VII, perhaps the most famous of all statements of papal claims and prerogatives

Christian dogma of passive obedience and non-resistance. As one of his most penetrating critics pointed out, 'Christ alone, in unison with God, can give and take away dominion, according to the scriptures; but Hildebrand teaches that he himself has authority over kings and kingdoms.' It is perhaps true that Gregory nowhere explicitly rejects the old doctrine, enunciated by pope Gelasius I (492–96), that the world should be ruled in harmony by the two powers, the sacred authority of the priesthood and the royal power. But contemporaries soon concluded that this was what he was doing in practice. 'Behold,' wrote one, 'and see how Hildebrand and his bishops, resisting God's ordinance, wish to destroy and bring to nothing the two powers by which the world is ruled. . . . They desire all bishops to be like themselves (who are no true bishops at all), and wish for kings through whom and with whose consent they may themselves rule.'

At the same time there was a steady encroachment on the autonomy of the episcopacy. Gregory's interpretation of papal headship in the church, his intervention through legates and through his powers of jurisdiction in the affairs of the national churches, brought him into conflict with other Catholic bishops and metropolitans, who, rightly or wrongly, regarded his monarchical pretensions as an attack on the canonically ordained order. No one fought back more stubbornly than Manasses, archbishop of Rheims, who struggled hard for independence for five years; but throughout Gaul, Lombardy and Germany the episcopate was up in arms. 'This dangerous man', wrote the archbishop of Bremen, 'wants to order the bishops about as though they were servants on his estates; and if they do not do all his commands, they have to go to Rome, or else they are suspended without due process of law.' The archbishop of Cologne was more defiant. 'As the Roman bishop claims due obedience from the archbishop of Cologne,' he wrote, 'so the archbishop demands that the bishop of Rome refrain from interfering in canonical discipline within the archbishop's territory.' And when the German bishops withdrew obedience from Gregory at the beginning of 1076, their main complaint was that he had brought the divinely-appointed order which had hitherto existed among the members of Christ, into lamentable confusion. 'So far as lay in your power,' they told him, 'you have torn from the bishops' hands all the authority conferred on them through the grace of the Holy Spirit, who takes part in their ordination.'

Gregory VII's doctrines – and still more, perhaps, his fiery personality, with his passionate beliefs, his lack of tact, his forthright language and his distaste for compromise – embroiled him not only with most of the great prelates of Europe. By 1083 no fewer than thirteen of the cardinals had abandoned his cause in despair. There was scarcely a king or prince with whom he was on good terms. Only with William I of England did he maintain an uneasy peace, acquiescing in the Conqueror's power over the English church because William used his power to reform and to appoint reformatory bishops and abbots. Hence it was only after William's death in 1087 that conflict between the Anglo-Norman monarchy and the papacy broke out. With his Norman allies in Sicily, on the other hand, Gregory soon quarrelled, and Robert Guiscard was excommunicated. Even before his breach with Henry IV of Germany he denounced Philip I of France as a tyrant who incited his people to evil by the wicked example of his actions and morals. But the very novelty of Gregory's doctrines, and the extreme way in which he announced them, militated against success, and provoked a hostile reaction; they ran contrary to the general sentiment of what was reasonable and just. It was only where he found ready to hand an opposition which saw its own advantage in co-operating with the papacy that his intervention was effective. This was the case in Germany and Italy, and here there was a head-on collision between the empire and the papacy. The reason was that Henry IV gave his support, for reasons we have seen, to the German and Lombard national churches; and consequently the pope could secure control over the bishops and enforce the reforming decrees only by attacking the power of the monarchy, which was the backbone of resistance. But even here Gregory overreached himself. By 1083 or 1084 he was losing ground on all fronts, and at the time of his death Henry IV was everywhere in the ascendant.

Thus Gregory died a failure, without having achieved any of his objects. In spite of this he stands high in the history of the medieval papacy. His greatness, it is often said, lay not in what he achieved, but in the ideals which he passed on to his successors; far more than any of his predecessors, including Nicholas I, he set the papacy on the road to universal dominion and absolute theocratic power, and so it is possible to draw a straight line from what he set out, but failed, to do, to the exalted claims of Innocent III and Boniface VIII. But even this is less clear than at first sight appears. To begin with, it is striking, as Caspar has pointed out, that just as Gregory himself did not build upon the work of his great predecessors in the reform movement, cardinal Humbert and St Peter Damian, so the popes and canonists of later generations did not build upon his pronouncements. Few of his statements found a permanent place in the law of the church. Here, as elsewhere, he stands (in Caspar's phrase) 'by himself', a lonely figure, and the course of development passes him by. If we set out to trace the development of the papal monarchy, the names that stand out are not Gregory's but, in the eleventh century, Leo IX (1049–54) and Urban II (1088–99), and, in the twelfth century, Eugenius III (1145–53) and Alexander III (1159–81). These are the popes who laid the foundations of the papal monarchy; and by comparison with them Gregory's stormy pontificate appears almost as a distraction, if not a deviation.

Paradoxically, therefore, it might almost be said that Gregory VII led the church into a blind alley. The attempt to bring the state into subordination to the church, with its inevitable corollary, the immersion of the papacy in politics, brought about a strong reaction, in which the most influential reformers of the next generation played a leading part. No one was more outspokenly critical of the direction of papal policy than St Bernard, who became abbot of Clairvaux in 1118; but the whole Cistercian movement, with its hostility to study and particularly to the new canon law, and its respect for episcopal authority, which Gregory VII's policy had weakened, was a sign of the rejection of Gregorian pretensions. With the rise of Cîteaux reform was sought, once again, not by conquest of the world, but by flight from the world. Meanwhile, the consequences of Gregory's intemperate policies had to be liquidated; and this was the task of his successors down to, and including, Calixtus II (1119–24). Only when the conflicts of the Hildebrandine period were out of the way could the papacy proceed with the work of establishing its primacy within the church, which Leo IX had begun.

The reaction against Gregory VII's policies began immediately after his death. Whether or not his objects were right, it was obvious that his methods were wrong. Direct political action had not only failed to produce results, but had alienated the sympathy of the public, which could not swallow the idea that the pope's business was political. From these facts the papal curia, led by the cardinals, drew the necessary consequences, and Gregory's theocratic pretensions were hastily dropped. The abbot of Monte Cassino, a moderate man desirous above all else of a compromise peace, was elected pope as Victor III; and it was Henry IV's greatest mistake that he did not grasp the opportunity of Victor's short pontificate, in 1086 and 1087, to reach a settlement. On Victor's death the opportunity passed. His successor, Urban II (1088–99), was a totally different man. He was also a totally different man from Gregory VII, a great French nobleman as contrasted with the raw Tuscan farmer's son, an astute diplomatist carefully calculating the balance of political power, who avoided all Gregory's mistakes, above all else the exaggerated claims which immediately provoked resistance. But Urban was utterly determined to maintain the programme of the reform party – though not Gregory's pretensions to rule over kingdoms – and compromise was henceforward out of the question.

Urban II's pontificate was the turning-point in the struggle that had commenced in 1076. Coming to the throne at the lowest ebb of papal power, he saw clearly from the start that the papal position was unshakable, so long as he had the alliance of the Normans of Sicily, which Gregory had jeopardized. In fact, the sphere of influence of the papacy was far wider than it had been at the time of Henry III's death. As a result of the Norman conquest, southern Italy had been forcibly converted from Orthodox to Latin Christianity, and now for the first time since the eighth century owed obedience to the pope. The Christian conquest of Spain worked in the same direction; Alexander II had formed connections with the Christian kings and princes of Spain similar to those entered into with the Normans in southern Italy, treating them as vassals of the papacy, and the Christian troops were followed by Cluniac monks, who set to work to destroy the national Mozarabic rites and to substitute those of Rome. And England also was 'a new acquisition', won over to the cause of reform by force of arms, for William the Conqueror's expedition in 1066 had been blessed by the pope, and William himself provided with a holy standard, as though he were embarking on a crusade against the enemies of the church. Thus southern and western Europe was taking shape as a religious and cultural unity linked with the reform papacy; and from this foundation Urban II was able to face with equanimity the opposition of the German king. Driven from Italy, he found refuge in France, where he quickly reached an understanding with the Capetian dynasty; and from this basis he gradually and skilfully built up the standing of the papacy, finally gathering round him the chivalry of Europe – to the exclusion of the German emperor – in the First Crusade (1096).

The First Crusade has been described, not without reason, as 'the foreign policy of the reformed papacy.' It set the pope, in place of the emperor, at the head of Europe, and assured the papacy a moral leadership. In this way Urban II's cool, resolute guidance gradually brought about a reversal in the position of the parties, while his diplomacy and tact recovered for the church the sympathy which Gregory VII's intransigence had lost. Henry IV, rather than the pope, seemed now to be the obstinate, uncompromising party; and in Germany the feeling grew that he alone stood between the kingdom and peace. After 1097, when he returned unsuccessfully from Italy, he felt the ground slipping away from under his feet, and offered

equum fo fcau
cu qui fedeb uc
fup eum :. b eb
c la dium ·

uum aluum
qui fedebac
ip eu mabo
ca a rcu m

37 Knights in armour at the time of the First Crusade (1096); from an early twelfth-century Spanish manuscript

repeatedly to discuss terms of settlement. But now the church, in its new-found strength, was the uncompromising party, and his offers were rejected. Finally, in 1104, his son rose in rebellion, convinced that Henry was ruining the monarchy's last chance to save itself; and Henry IV's death in 1106 left his rebellious son in control. Henry V began negotiations with the papacy immediately in 1107 – the year of the settlement of the investiture controversy in France – but even with the change of ruler it proved difficult to reach a basis of agreement, and it was only in 1122 that the concordat of Worms brought the struggle to an end.

The concordat of Worms was in no way a final settlement of the conflict of church and state. No formal settlement could dispose of the problems arising from the twofold loyalties of bishops and prelates. But it did provide a basis for peaceful co-existence after fifty years of strife, and to that extent it marks the end of one period and the beginning of another. The course of the struggle had shown that the full theocratic claims enunciated by Gregory VII were not only unobtainable, but ran contrary to general sentiment. Therefore the major questions which had been in the forefront in 1075 and 1076 were tacitly dropped and the issue was narrowed to the more limited question of investitures. It is unnecessary to discuss in detail the terms of the settlement, or of the parallel settlements with France and England nego-tiated in 1107. In general, it may be said that they were an attempt to draw the boundaries between church and state and so to reach an equilibrium. There were to be many more conflicts of church and state during the middle ages; but henceforward they would arise not – as in the days of Gregory VII – over matters of principle, but over the disputed frontiers between the two spheres, or over territorial problems in Italy. The papacy was jealous of its rights and would not suffer encroachments; but from 1122 onwards it con-centrated its attention on its own sphere. The idea of reducing the state to dependence on the church had been rejected, just as much as the idea of reducing the church to dependence on the state; and the twelfth-century papacy drew the logical conclusion.

The change has never been better expressed than in Haller's words: 'the subjugation of the world is given up, and instead all efforts are concen-trated on the subordination of the church.' From the beginning of the twelfth to the end of the thirteenth centuries this becomes the daily concern of the popes. As Rudolf von Heckel once wrote, the world-wide dominion of the papacy rested not so much on its actions in the great field of politics as on the multitude of constantly repeated, day-by-day transactions – indi-vidually of small importance, but precisely because of their individual in-significance all the more impressive as a body – which made its authority a reality. In this development Gregory VII was not prominent; it was after his death, in the period reaching from Urban II to Alexander III, that it gathered pace. By the time of the Third Lateran Council (1179) at the close of Alexander III's pontificate, the outlines of the papal monarchy had taken shape. This was a revolution of the first magnitude which radically altered the place of the papacy in the church.

THE GROWTH OF PAPAL GOVERNMENT

One reason for the setbacks of Gregory VII was the rudimentary nature of the administrative organization at the pope's disposal. It was too autocratic and too narrowly based. The first generation of reformers had assumed that all that was necessary to set the church on a new course was a change of personnel at the top. It was in this spirit that Leo IX called in reformers from outside, such as Humbert of Moyenmoutier. The result was to inaugurate a radical change in the position of the Roman cardinals, particularly the cardinal-bishops, who ceased to be essentially religious dignitaries, concerned primarily with liturgical duties in the Lateran basilica and other churches of Rome, and became the pope's political advisers, or, as St Peter Damian said, 'spiritual senators of the universal church'. Leo IX's pontificate also marked an important stage in the creation of a new papal secretariat, free from Roman ties, which took over most of the political correspondence, now becoming an increasingly important part of papal business. But otherwise the old organs of administration, dating back in many cases to the seventh century and beyond, went on functioning as before, so far as they had not been disrupted in the anarchy of the preceding age. The rising importance of the cardinal-bishops was registered by the electoral decree of 1059, and there is evidence that Gregory VII tried to improve the efficiency of the existing organization, particularly on the financial side; but he made no innovations in the structure of papal government.

There were, of course, good reasons for this slowness in developing new organs of administration. In the first place, the early reformers could hardly have been expected to perceive the need for radical change. The centralization which became so characteristic a feature of church government after the beginning of the twelfth century was not part of a deliberate programme, planned from the start. Rather the reformers – Gregory VII no less than his predecessors – assumed that the bishops, once they were made aware of the ancient law of the church, would see the light and co-operate voluntarily in the work of reform. It was only when these hopes proved false that the papacy was driven to intervene directly on an ever-increasing scale in the affairs of the national churches, and an urgent need arose to adapt the machinery of government to the new circumstances. This occurred under Urban II (1088–99), whose pontificate thus stands out, in this as in other respects, as a decisive turning-point in papal history.

The factor which made reorganization unavoidable was the conflict which broke out in 1075. If Gregory VII retained the old administrative system intact, it was, no doubt, because, as the first Roman to become pope since 1045, he saw no reason to tamper with it. He had himself risen high in the papal bureaucracy, and in any case he was not temperamentally the man to bother with administrative reform; 'the details of the chancery,' as Poole observed, 'did not interest him.' Still less was he the man to share his powers. His opponents complained that 'he removed the cardinals from the councils of the holy see'. Certainly, under Gregory the developments which had begun before 1073 came to a standstill, if they were not actually reversed. But these very facts produced a reaction. By 1082 discontent among the cardinals was rife. In 1084 a large number, particularly among the cardinal-priests, abandoned Gregory and went over to his opponent, pope Clement III (1080–1100). So also did virtually the whole of the old administrative organization, including the seven *iudices de clero*, its traditional heads, the chancellor, and the *scriniarii*, who were responsible for the preparation of papal documents. Thus, by the time of Gregory's death in 1085, the old administrative system had in effect collapsed. At the same time, the long struggle between pope and anti-pope for control of Rome produced further developments. Clement III, in particular, in order to gain support, made concessions to the cardinal-priests which put them on the level of the cardinal-bishops; he also raised the deacons of the Roman church to the same rank. By the time of his death in 1100 the cardinals were emerging as a college or corporate body.

When Urban II succeeded in 1088, it was necessary to take cognizance of these facts. By now a thoroughgoing reorganization was unavoidable, and no one could have been better suited than Urban for the task. A French nobleman, who had been a monk at Cluny, he had the advantage of acquaintance both with Cluniac organization and with the feudal administration of Capetian France. Urban's model for the reform of papal administration was the royal court or household, as it existed at the time in France or Anglo-Norman England; he wished to give the papacy a similar monarchical form of government. He was, therefore, in a very real sense the creator of the papal curia, and it is no accident that he was the first pope who used the word *curia* as the official designation for the central government of the church.

With the emergence of the curia a new chapter of papal history begins. Naturally, the development of appropriate institutions took something like a generation to complete; but it would be difficult to exaggerate the importance of the changes Urban II inaugurated. The establishment of the curia as the pivot of the administration put the papacy on an equal footing with the rising states of feudal Europe; while at the same time the new conception of the pope's government as a court – for *curia*, as in the contemporary secular states, meant both the central administration as a whole and a court of law – prepared the ground for the legal developments which contributed so much to the rise of the papal monarchy. Here again, as Fournier pointed out, the pontificate of Urban II marked a decisive turning-point. Under Gregory VII, and as the result of the researches which he initiated, many ancient texts, genuine and apocryphal, had been brought to light, which could be used to bolster papal authority. But their immediate impact was small, and it was not until Urban II set out the principles of interpretation that the first steps were taken towards organizing the new material scientifically and shaping it into a coherent legal system. Urban's principles were applied and developed by the canonists Ivo of Chartres and Alger of Liège; and finally, about 1140, the Bolognese monk, Gratian, produced his *Concordia discordantium canonum*, or (as it was soon called) *Decretum*, which, with its emphasis on the pope's legislative and dispensing powers, became the starting-point for the development of ecclesiastical law in the twelfth century.

Urban II's administrative innovations can be quickly summarized. They affected all the main branches of the curia, the writing-office, which was later to develop into the chancery, the chapel, the financial organization, and, first and foremost, the position of the cardinals, whose new responsibilities were symbolized by the practice, still infrequent under Urban himself, but rapidly becoming the rule under his successor, Paschal II (1099–1118), of appending their autograph signatures, or subscriptions, at the foot of papal privileges. The decisive fact was that Urban II accepted, where Gregory VII had resisted, the new position which the cardinals had acquired since the days of Leo IX. Under him the college of cardinals began to take over functions – such as the excommunication of kings and bishops, or the decision of disputed episcopal elections – which earlier popes had reserved for the synods. It had emerged, in other words, as the pope's supreme advisory body, fulfilling the same function as the king's council in England or France, and participating at the highest level in decisions of policy and in the government of the church.

Closely connected with this fundamental change in the position of the cardinals was the rise of the papal chapel. Increasingly immersed in political duties, the cardinals were no longer free to perform their traditional religious functions, and these were now assigned to chaplains. They are first specifically mentioned under Paschal II, but there is no reason to doubt that the institution of the papal chapel, on the model of the chapels at the courts of secular rulers, was the work of Urban II. He also carried out a thorough reorganization of the papal finances, which was long overdue. Here, without much doubt, his model was Cluny, and the first papal chamberlain, or *camerarius*, who functioned under both Urban and Paschal, was a monk

38 Part of the first page of a copy of Gratian's *Decretum* written at Bologna in the twelfth century; the text is on the left and 'glosses' (or legal comments) have been added in various hands in the margin on the right

from Cluny, named Peter. In many respects, the foundation of the *camera*, which quickly displaced the old organs of financial administration, was the most important of Urban II's innovations. Finally, the pope's secretarial arrangements were reorganized by John of Gaeta, who became Urban II's chancellor in 1089 and retained the office for thirty years, until he himself became pope, as Gelasius II, in 1118. John of Gaeta standardized the forms of the papal privilege, renovated its style, introduced the new curial minuscule script, and made important innovations in dating. But these formal details, indicative though they are of the new spirit infusing the administration, are less important in the present context than two changes in organization. The first is that the head of the organization, i.e., the chancellor, was henceforward regularly a cardinal, who normally held his post for life, or until he became pope. Secondly, the Roman *scriniarii*, who had formerly staffed the office, were finally displaced. Their last occurrence is under Calixtus II (1119–24); but it is fair to say that it was during the chancellorship of John of Gaeta that the pope was finally equipped with 'a personal staff of clerks to take the place of the notaries whom he found on the spot.' Well might Poole write of John of Gaeta's term of office that it was 'a memorable landmark'.

The importance of the changes introduced under Urban II needs no emphasis. The key was the close personal dependence of the new offices on the pope himself. The *camera*, in particular, was concerned in the first instance with the income flowing directly into the pope's private purse, rather than with the revenues of the Roman church. The early *camerarii* were men in the pope's confidence, acting on his orders. As such they rose rapidly. Under Eugenius III (1145–53), the office was so important that it was confided to a cardinal. The English pope, Hadrian IV (1154–59), placed another Englishman, Boso, in charge, and under Boso, who himself became a cardinal in 1156, the *camera* finally became the central financial organ, displacing the old offices of *arcarius* and *saccellarius* and extending its control over the estates and patrimonies of the Roman church. It may, indeed, be said that it was Boso who initiated the policy of territorial recuperation and expansion which was the main cause of the great conflicts of empire and papacy under Alexander III and Innocent III. The rise in the importance of the office of chancellor was equally rapid. Not only pope Gelasius II, but

39 Pope Paschal II (1099–1118), whose attempt to settle the dispute over investitures by renouncing the church's regalities, was repudiated by the prelates; marginal drawing from a contemporary Italian manuscript

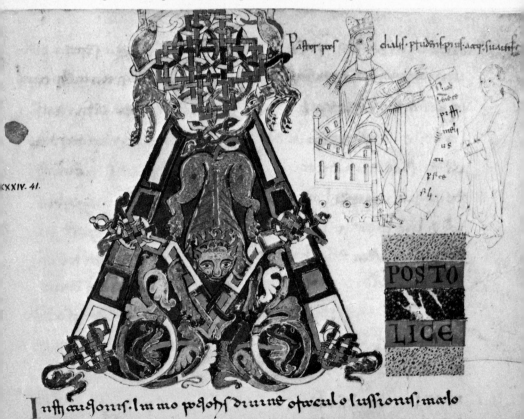

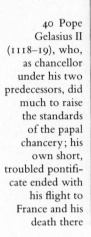

40 Pope Gelasius II (1118–19), who, as chancellor under his two predecessors, did much to raise the standards of the papal chancery; his own short, troubled pontificate ended with his flight to France and his death there

also Lucius II, Alexander III and Gregory VIII, had previously been chancellors, a clear indication of the high standing of the office in the twelfth century. And even Urban II's organization of the papal chapel was a more important development than may appear at first glance. Like the kings of England and France and the German emperors, the popes used their chaplains for a wide variety of duties – particularly as scribes or *scriptores* – so that they quickly became, in effect, the main reservoir of clerical and administrative labour. Their importance is sufficiently indicated by the fact that Paschal II raised no fewer than nine of his *capellani et scriptores* to the rank of cardinal. Without them the rapid expansion of the central administration in the twelfth century would scarcely have been possible.

The keystone of the new curia was the college of cardinals. Cardinals now acted as departmental heads in the *camera* and chancery, and from the time of Paschal II papal legates were nearly always chosen from their ranks. Both these functions enabled them to keep their finger on the pulse of the church. But more important was their collegiate activity. When the word 'consistory' first began to be used for their meetings is not certain – perhaps not before the pontificate of Eugenius III (1145–53) – but already under Paschal II, if not under Urban II, they were meeting together as a body to decide

99

important issues and advise the pope. After Paschal's death in 1118 the cardinals met 'in common' to negotiate about the new election. But even earlier, in 1111 and 1112, we find them playing a decisive part in the negotiations between Paschal and the emperor Henry V. No less important was their intervention in the protracted negotiations which began in 1119 and finally led to the conclusion of the concordat of Worms in 1122. They were also consulted on matters of faith, which previously would have been reserved for a synod – it was on the advice of the cardinals, for example, that Innocent II condemned the teachings of Peter Abelard in 1141 – and, more generally, on the ever-increasing number of 'causæ maiores'. It was, in fact, the college of cardinals which ensured continuity in papal policy from pontificate to pontificate. As the work of the curia increased, particularly after the pontificate of Innocent II (1130–43), the pope could not do without their active co-operation; but this very fact assured them an independent position. This they made clear in 1148 when the cardinals believed that pope Eugenius III was taking sides with his old teacher, St Bernard, against the famous theologian, Gilbert de la Porrée. They were, they said, the hinges (*cardines*) of the church, and they advised the pope not to act without them and not to forget that it was to them, 'the hinges round which the whole church revolves', that he owed his promotion; nothing, they maintained, should be finally decided 'sine nostra auctoritate'.

The developments inaugurated by Urban II may be said to have been completed in all essentials by 1130. Naturally, the various departments continued to evolve. The writing-office, in particular, grew in size, as the administrative and judicial activity of the curia expanded. Under Alexander III (1159–81), probably early in his pontificate, the personnel was graded into categories, the seven notaries at the top and the ordinary copy-clerks, or scribes, below them. Before the end of the century another category had appeared, the abbreviators, who drafted letters which did not fit into one or other of the normal types. And by 1185 the 'chancery' – the term first begins to be used under Lucius III (1181–85) – hitherto part of the undifferentiated papal household, had 'gone out of court' and become a separate department. These developments were a response to growing commitments and an increasing volume of work. Their object was greater efficiency. But the essential change was the creation of the *curia Romana* on the model of the feudal court. Contemporaries were well aware of the revolution in papal government which this implied, and many did not like it. Gerhoh of Reichersberg pointed out in 1158 that there was no warrant in the ancient records for describing the holy see as a court; it was a 'blot' on the reputation of the Roman church that it allowed itself to be called by such a name.

A decade earlier St Bernard had made even more pointed criticisms of the direction in which things were moving. He angrily denounced the new role of the cardinals and grimly described how the pope's palace resounded with legal altercation, 'but Justinian's law, not the Lord's'. What could be more unworthy for the pope than to spend almost every hour of every day on business of that sort? Bernard's criticisms of the curia were not exceptional. They were echoed by John of Salisbury, Ulrich of Steinfeld, Stephen of Tournai and Peter of Blois, to name only a few of the better known writers. But their effect was minimal. The clock could not be put back, nor the wheels reversed. The transformation initiated by Urban II, the rise of the Roman curia and what is sometimes called the 'institutionalization' of papal government, set the tone for the succeeding generation. From Innocent II (1130–43) to Innocent IV (1243–54) the main thread in papal history was the erection of the papal monarchy on foundations laid by Urban II.

THE POPES OF THE TWELFTH CENTURY

By 1130 the age of reform had come to an end. The concordat of Worms in 1122 inaugurated a forty years' period of peace between empire and papacy, and with the conclusion of the long struggle new issues quickly came to the fore. Already in 1124, on the death of Calixtus II, the cardinals were deeply divided, and it looked as if there would be a schism. In 1130 the schism actually came about, a majority of the cardinals electing Anacletus II (1130–38), while a strong minority supported his rival, Innocent II (1130–43). The schism of 1130, commonly attributed to the pressure of aristocratic factions in Rome, was in fact the result of a conflict between the older generation of reformers, around Anacletus, who wished to exploit the victory for which they had fought so hard, and a younger generation, mostly raised to the purple after 1122, who were prepared to abide by the compromise solution and profit from the restoration of peaceful conditions in order to build up the papacy's control of the church and restore its territorial position in Italy. The victory of Innocent II ensured the preponderance of this element, and the tendencies they represented continued to dominate papal policy until the renewal of conflict with the empire after the election of Alexander III in 1159.

The post-reform period was ushered in by the Lateran council held in 1123. This was the first ecumenical council since the council of Constantinople in 869, and the first to be held in the west under the aegis of the pope;

it was also the first ecumenical council the decrees of which were promulgated by the pope in his own name. The very decision to summon it was programmatic. With the conclusion of the concordat of Worms the papacy had emancipated itself from imperial control and asserted its position as an independent political power. The purpose of the council was to celebrate this triumph. It also registered the papacy's success in establishing universal dominion over the Catholic church. The independence of the great metropolitans was broken. The distinguished French canonist, bishop Ivo of Chartres, told the archbishop of Sens in no uncertain terms that the judgments of the holy see were irrevocable and that anyone who opposed them exposed himself *ipso facto* to a charge of heresy. And Paschal II threatened archbishop Ralph of Canterbury with excommunication simply because, without consulting the pope, he had decided important cases, 'which ought to be judged by us'.

From the time of Innocent II (1130–43) the new spirit permeated the curia. Innocent was the first pope to reserve a whole class of cases – namely, violent assault against a cleric or monk – for the pope's own dispensation. He was also the first pope, so far as we know, who intervened directly to secure the grant of a benefice for a particular clerk. Innocent's intervention took the form of a request, or recommendation, to the appropriate authority – in this particular instance, the archbishop of Compostella – but already by the time of Eugenius III (1145–53) it is evident that the pope was

41 Popes and anti-popes. This sixteenth-century sketch of frescoes which used to be in the chamber of secret councils in the old Lateran palace shows, at left, popes Gregory VII and Victor III, with the anti-pope Clement III at Gregory's feet; at right, the crouching anti-pope Gregory VIII (familiarly 'Burdinus', or 'the Spanish ass') receives a copy of the concordat of Worms in the presence of pope Calixtus II

42 The crowning of Lothar III as emperor (1133) in the Lateran by pope Innocent II, whom he supported against Anacletus II. This too was the subject of a fresco in the Lateran palace, and is shown here in a sixteenth-century drawing

claiming special rights in a particular category of benefices – namely, those vacated by newly appointed bishops – and by the time of Hadrian IV (1154–59), under whom 'papal provisions' (as they came to be called) were relatively frequent, recommendations were giving way to orders. A generation later, under Lucius III (1181–85), the pope appointed executors to see that his orders were carried out, and Celestine III (1191–98) used the weapon of ecclesiastical censure to beat down resistance.

The step-by-step extension of papal control over ecclesiastical benefices is a characteristic example of the trend of twelfth-century developments. It could be paralleled in many other fields. It would be quite wrong to regard it as a process of deliberate encroachment or aggressive centralization. Once the papacy had emerged successful from the Investiture contest, few people disputed its place at the head of the church. The rights for which it had struggled were set out by Gratian in the *Decretum* which he completed shortly after the Second Lateran Council of 1139; and through the *Decretum*, which was almost immediately accepted as an authoritative statement of the current law, they became (in Haller's words) 'the creed of the century'. Gratian had no doubt or hesitation about the pope's omnipotence, or about the precedence of church law over secular law. For him, the pope's decretals were not merely equal, but superior, to the canons of the ecumenical councils, for the pope could interpret the canons and dispense from them, just as he could revoke privileges. All were subordinate to the overriding

103

authority of the holy see; and it is no accident that, beginning with Celestine II (1143–44), the clause *salva sedis apostolicæ auctoritate* was regularly included in all papal privileges. It expressed the pope's supreme legislative authority, or at least his power to make law or modify law, not so much by legislative enactment as by settling doubtful points of interpretation and by the decision of concrete cases.

— Through his attitude towards papal supremacy and his support for the pope's judicial authority, Gratian laid the foundation for the rapid expansion of papal power which followed. Nothing was more urgently needed, after the upheavals of the preceding century, than an authority which could give a final ruling on the current state of the law. Every aspect of Christian life and ecclesiastical organization – marriage, ordination, sacraments, patronage, canonization, electoral procedure, to name but a few – needed definition. That is why recourse to Rome and to the processes of the Roman curia grew at so phenomenal a speed after the pontificate of Innocent II. The advantages the pope's authority conferred were too manifest to be neglected. Hence, as one historian has said, there was 'no need for the popes to seek for business; they were overwhelmed by it'. Or, as another historian has written, 'the principle of authority, which was grounded finally in the bishops of Rome, was in its inception as much the creation of provincial ecclesiastics as of the papacy itself'. Even in the case of papal provisions the initiative came from the petitioners rather than from the pope, particularly from the new class of university-trained clerks; and it is significant that one of the first to benefit by papal intervention was the famous *magister sententiarum*, Peter Lombard, whom Eugenius III recommended to the bishop of Beauvais. The result, in any case, was a flood of appeals to Rome and, perhaps more significant still, a growing tendency to cut out the lower instances and take cases and lawsuits direct to the papal curia.

This flood of new business had two consequences, both of great importance in the growth of the papal monarchy. The first was to force forward the development of the administrative machinery, both in the curia and outside. By the time of Eugenius III and Hadrian IV the methods used a generation earlier were becoming antiquated. In particular, the papal legates simply could not cope. They continued, of course, to function at the highest level, negotiating with kings and giving a lead to local prelates in synods. But side by side with them a new system of delegate-judges was instituted. The delegates were usually commissions of local churchmen, three in number, vested with papal authority to decide a particular case or to ascertain the facts and refer them to the curia for the pope's decision. The system of delegates, controlled from the curia, quickly became a characteristic feature of papal government, and before the end of the century they were operating in scores and hundreds in every country of Catholic Europe. The second consequence was legal. As more and more cases came before the pope for judgment, his decisions, usually conveyed in decretals, often resulted in substantial changes or modifications in the law. Hence the decretals were avidly collected – more than fifty distinct collections were circulating between 1170 and 1210 – and the result was the rapid obsolescence of the old law and the rise of a new law emanating directly from the pope. Already, for example, in the summary of Gratian's *Decretum* written by Simon de Bisigniano between 1174 and 1179, no less than eighty new decretals were used, and it has been calculated that, all in all, the compilers accumulated more than a thousand letters of Innocent III's predecessors. Thus arose what Sicard of Cremona, writing in or around 1180, called the *novum ius canonicum*, a new law which was papal in origin and papal in spirit, and which paved the way for the exercise by later popes of the legislative power, for, as Maitland wrote, only 'a fine line' divided 'the declaration of law' from 'open legislation'.

These developments, though they had begun earlier, are associated preeminently with the long pontificate of Alexander III (1159–81), himself a distinguished lawyer who had taught in the university of Bologna and, as already mentioned, had occupied the key position of chancellor for six years prior to his elevation to the papal throne. It is certainly no accident that of the thousand decretals selected for preservation and comment as important contributions to church law no less than 713 were issued by Alexander. Nevertheless, we know tantalizingly little in detail of the actual measures taken by Alexander III to strengthen and develop the government of the church. It seems likely that he reinforced the organization of the chancery to cope with the growing volume of business passing through it; in all probability he was responsible for the division between ordinary letters of justice, which went out under a simplified procedure, and letters which had first to be submitted to the pope for his approval and assent. The object of this distinction was evidently to relieve the pope of the growing body of routine work. How successful it was is another question. Under Alexander III the pope sat in consistory with the cardinals every day of the week, mainly in order to hear and decide law suits, and it was not until the pontificate of Innocent III that the number of consistories was reduced to three a week. By this time a good deal of the judicial work was being handed over to the pope's chaplains, many of them trained lawyers; but this practice does not seem to have been introduced before the very end of the twelfth century.

In these circumstances, it is not surprising that the character of the curia changed, and also the character of the popes. Not only Alexander III but also Gregory VIII and Innocent III were lawyers by training, and so were a high proportion of the cardinals. As has frequently been observed, there was no saint among the twelfth-century popes. The complaints to which this diversion of the papacy from religious to legal functions gave rise have already been mentioned. They commence with St Bernard and never cease thereafter. They are directed against 'the inextricable forest of papal decretals' confusing the old law of the church, against the wiles and avarice of the advocates gathered like vultures at the entrance to the Lateran palace, but above all against the immersion of the pope in legal business. 'What is it', St Bernard asked Eugenius III, 'to litigate or listen to litigants from morning to night?' There has been a good deal of controversy about these complaints and how far they were justified. One thing that is certain is that the pope was harassed and burdened by what he called 'a multiplicity of affairs'. When a serious error occurred in one of his rescripts, Alexander III excused himself to the archbishop of Canterbury on the grounds that 'it arose from our being overworked'.

An important factor contributing to this state of affairs was the renewal of conflict between empire and papacy after the accession of Alexander III in 1159. It was only to be expected that the German emperors, once they

43 St Bernard, relentless critic of the new developments in the Roman curia during the pontificate of his pupil, pope Eugenius III; from a thirteenth-century painting

44, 45 The leaden seal or 'bull' of Eugenius III (1145–53). Right, gilded reliquary bearing the features of Frederick Barbarossa

had put their house in order at home, would seek to restore the imperial position in Italy, which had crumbled during the Investiture contest. After the accession of Frederick Barbarossa in 1152 the time for such an effort was ripe. Almost inevitably, it led to conflict with the papacy which also, from the time of Eugenius III, had been trying to put its house in order, reorganize its estates, assert its authority in Rome, where a commune had been set up in 1143, and above all to consolidate its hold over the so-called 'Matildine lands' – that is to say, the properties of Matilda, countess of Tuscany, which she had donated to the papacy on her death in 1115. Not surprisingly Frederick refused to recognize the validity of this donation. He was also determined to restore the sovereignty over Rome which the Ottonian emperors had exercised, and to exercise the old imperial rights – going back to Lothar's constitution of 824 – in the papal patrimonies outside Rome. Though the emperor, as was to be expected, sought to justify his position by theoretical arguments and raised up a number of anti-popes, the conflict between Frederick I and Alexander III was very different in character from that between Henry IV and Gregory VII. It was essentially a struggle for territorial power in Italy, in which no fundamental principles were involved, unless it was held to be a fundamental principle that the papacy, to safeguard its independence, must rule an independent territory; and if Alexander emerged successful, it was less through his own efforts than through those of the Lombard communes, which had reasons of their own for opposing the emperor.

The conflict was brought to an end in 1177 by the treaty of Venice. As in 1122, the papacy had to be content with a compromise; for if Frederick practically gave up his claim to sovereignty over the papal lands round Rome, by way of compensation he remained master of the German church, and his schismatic bishops were left in possession of their sees. Here was clear evidence of the limitations in practice of the universal monarchy which the pope possessed in theory. In addition, the long struggle imposed an intolerable strain on the papacy. In 1162 Alexander had been forced to abandon Italy and take refuge in France, and with Italy he perforce abandoned a goodly part of the papal revenues. In 1173 he had to send an envoy to England to whip round among the English prelates for voluntary gifts to help him out; he had already done the same more than once in France. By the time of his death in 1181 the papacy was in dire financial straits, and Alexander III left his successors a heavy burden of debt.

Inevitably the standards of the administration suffered. While expenses mounted in response to the demand for more government, money to pay the growing staff was not available. Very few of the officials at the curia drew a salary; for the most part they lived on fees, but because fees were not fixed, the door lay wide open to bribery and corruption. There was nothing new about this. Ivo of Chartres, writing under Paschal II, had complained of the cupidity of the pope's domestic staff, and under Celestine II or Lucius II there seem to have been proposals for reform, in which Eugenius III, at that time abbot of St Anastasius in Rome, had a hand. But nothing came of them. The practice of papal provision originated almost certainly as a means of providing for the clerks of the curia, and this was one main reason for its extension. Hadrian IV claimed the right to dispose of the benefices of clerks who died at the curia; Alexander III began the practice of granting 'expectancies' to benefices not yet vacant, although he himself specifically forbade this abuse at the Third Lateran Council in 1179. But none of these expedients solved the problem, and by the end of Alexander's pontificate the reputation of the curia was at a low level. The last twenty or twenty-five years of the twelfth century were the time when the most pungent satires on the corruption and avarice of the curia were written –

46 Representation
of a *concilium* from
an eleventh-century
collection of canons

including the notorious 'Gospel according to the Mark of Silver' and the
legend of the blessed martyrs Albinus (silver) and Rufinus (gold) – and almost the first task Innocent III found awaiting him when he became pope
in 1198, was to root out a ring of forgers operating in the papal chancery
or its purlieus.

The evils and abuses which were undermining respect for the curia under
Alexander III became fully evident after his death in 1181. The popes between Alexander III and Innocent III have often been depicted as old, tired
men, chosen for their complaisance and too feeble either to maintain
Alexander's firm line towards the emperor or to check abuses. This is not a
true picture of the situation. In reality, the overtly political attitude of
Alexander III produced a reaction among the cardinals, who now, by a
decree of the Third Lateran council (1179), were firmly in control of papal
elections. It was a reaction against involvement in politics similar in character to that which had followed Gregory's VII's pontificate. Another factor
was the parlous situation in the Christian east, where Islam was going from
strength to strength. In 1187 Saladin occupied Jerusalem. How misguided
in such a situation for the papacy to waste its strength in wars with Frederick ! In any case, Alexander's policies, which had cost the church so
much, morally and materially, had not been more than half successful. An
influential party among the cardinals repudiated them. It included Albert

109

of Morra (the future pope Gregory VIII), the cardinal Hyacinth (later pope Celestine III), John Colonna, the first papal penitentiary (whom Celestine designated, unsuccessfully, as his successor), and Cencius, the head of the *camera* (later pope Honorius III), and it was deeply influenced by Cistercian ideals. It was, in effect, a 'peace' party, though not a party of peace at any price; that is to say, it took the view that the papacy should be content with its pre-eminence *ratione peccati* and not strive for direct political power, should maintain peaceful relations with the empire, and should concentrate, above all else, on the urgent tasks of reform.

It was this party which was responsible for the election of Lucius III (1181-85), a man of outstanding probity and essentially a man of peace. On Lucius' death there was something of a reaction against his compliance towards the emperor, though no party wanted a renewal of conflict, and Urban III (1185-87), a man of fiery temperament, was chosen. But on Urban's death after a pontificate of only twenty-three months, the moderates again gained the upper hand, and Albert of Morra, the chancellor, who had been a cardinal since 1156, was chosen as pope Gregory VIII (1187). Gregory was known to be in high esteem with the emperor Frederick. His real concern was the crusade and moral reform. In face of the new perils confronting it – not least of all, the heresies which were growing more powerful every day in reaction against the worldliness of the clergy – the church, Gregory said, required the co-operation of princes. In the short eight weeks during which he reigned, Gregory set about reform in earnest. Among other things he forced the cardinals to agree to desist from the practice of accepting 'gifts' from suppliants. The result, on his death, was a sharp reaction and the election of Clement III (1187-91), a Roman. Clement's pontificate was marked by a decided change of temper. Gregory VIII's reforms were buried, all his notaries were removed from the chancery, and the Cistercian influence, represented by cardinal Henry of Albano, was frozen out. Few popes before the period of the Renaissance had a greater money-hunger than Clement III, and there is no doubt that under him bribery and corruption flourished. When he died in 1191, the position was such that no one wanted the tiara, until finally the oldest of the cardinals, Hyacinth, was persuaded to accept office, 'lest there should be a schism'.

When he became pope as Celestine III (1191-98), Hyacinth had been a cardinal for forty-seven years and was already eighty-five years old. He had a high reputation, was pacific, incorruptible and a learned theologian. What he feared, above all else, was the growth of materialism in the church, and at an earlier stage in his career he had opposed war with Frederick I

47 Pope Celestine III crowning Henry VI emperor in Rome (1191); ▶
from a contemporary chronicle

ihparor

ihparor · celestin' · eccłia beati peti

pmo manu ungit · secdo bracha · tertio ho · eg · pp·

scrisma

octo virga · scto anulus · ultimo urtut·

precisely because – as proved to be the case – it would bring materialism in its train. In different circumstances he might have been the man to give the curia the new orientation it so badly needed. But circumstances were against him. The uneasy peace with the empire was breaking down. Celestine still tried to maintain a working agreement with Frederick I's successor, Henry VI, whom he crowned emperor in Rome in 1191; but when Henry conquered Sicily in 1194, consolidated his hold over central Italy, including the disputed Matildine lands, and his officials began to encroach on papal territories in the vicinity of Rome, the strained situation was evidently nearing breaking-point. In fact, Celestine carefully avoided a rupture down to Henry's death in 1197; on the other hand, he was too astute and experienced to give anything away. But the deterioration in relations gave the militant party among the cardinals the upper hand, and when Celestine died on 8 January 1198 they rejected the pope's designated successor, John Colonna, and chose instead the youngest of the cardinals, Lothar of Segni.

The election of Lothar of Segni, who took the name of Innocent III, was a programmatic step. If John Colonna, soon to be St Francis' earliest friend at the curia, was passed over, it was because the cardinals had decided that the situation required not the most religious but the strongest candidate available. As so often in the history of the papacy, the election of a Roman was a sign of gathering stormclouds. So it had been in 752 and 1073; so it was in 1198. Innocent III was only thirty-seven when he ascended the papal throne. A member of a noble Roman family, he had been made cardinal by his uncle, Clement III, in 1190, and perhaps for that reason had been cold-shouldered under Celestine III. The works he wrote during this interlude, *De contemptu mundi* and *De sacro altaris mysterio*, show him to have been a mediocre but safely orthodox theologian. But he had also studied law at Bologna, and law was clearly better suited to his great abilities, which were essentially practical. A born autocrat, Innocent's temperament was political and legal, and it is as a statesman and diplomat that he has gone down in history. This view perhaps does him less than justice. His concern for reform was real, and found expression, at the close of his pontificate, in the Fourth Lateran Council of 1215; and the outstanding evidence of his breadth of vision was the understanding he showed for St Francis, in spite of the opposition of the prelates. But he was also politician enough to grasp without hesitation the opportunity provided by the confusion in Germany after the death of Henry VI to break out of the stranglehold in which Henry's policies appeared to be imprisoning the papacy.

48 Pope Innocent III (1198–1216), scion of the noble family of the counts of Segni, who skilfully exploited the weakness of the empire after the death of Henry VI (1197) to establish the temporal power of the papacy

The pontificate of Innocent III is often regarded as the apogee of the medieval papacy, the culmination of the hierocratic tendencies for which Gregory VII had fought. Innocent III, it has been said, 'came nearest of all the popes towards realizing the theory of papal theocracy held by Nicholas I and Gregory VII'. How far Innocent's ideas were hierocratic in this sense, is another question. Historians have devoted a lot of time and effort to the analysis of Innocent III's views of the relations of church and state, and of empire and papacy. The conclusion most have reached is that he did not assert any claim to the direct exercise of political power, except, of course, within the papal states. He claimed a special authority in the case of the empire, on the grounds that the papacy had 'translated' the empire from the Greeks to the Franks. This was the papal theory of the empire which was already circulating in a less precise form in the ninth century. He also claimed feudal overlordship over certain kingdoms – Sicily, Aragon, Hungary, for example – which had placed themselves under papal protection; but the basis of this claim was not an abstract doctrine of *plenitudo potestatis*, but a carefully defined feudal prerogative. And, more generally, he claimed the right to interfere in secular affairs *ratione peccati* – that is to say, where sin might be committed. But this claim, though it might obviously be widely interpreted, was a very different thing from an outright theory of universal temporal sovereignty, or, in the parlance of the time, of the right to the 'two swords'.

But if it has to be said of Innocent III that 'he made no explicit claim to direct papal institution and control of the secular power' – that was to come, but not until Gregory IX (1227–41) or Innocent IV (1243–54) – he had no hesitation about his control over the church. 'So extensive', he wrote, 'is the authority of the apostolic see that nothing can reasonably be determined in all the affairs of the church except by its authority.' Innocent's weapon was the all-embracing doctrine of 'plenitude of power'. It was *ex plenitudine potestatis* that he asserted the exclusive right to authorize canonizations. He was also the first pope to claim the right to dispose of benefices by papal provision simply and solely by reason of his plenitude of power. But it is easy, if we make the pope's theoretical claims our sole standard of judgment, to exaggerate what the plenitude of power amounted to in practice. It was not merely that 'secular princes refused to accept Innocent's political claims at his own evaluation'. In purely ecclesiastical matters, also, 'his material resources were not sufficient to enforce his threats'. As a Catholic historian in England has recently written, 'the true weakness in the papal theory of sovereignty' was 'its failure to consider the executive', and this failure was no less characteristic of Innocent III than of lesser popes.

There is no clearer example of this weakness than the course of events in central Italy, though the same lack of an efficient executive is seen in Sicily, where Innocent took over government as guardian of the infant Frederick II. The result of Innocent's rule in Sicily was chaos, the rapid and total collapse of the strong government built up by the Norman kings. The position in the papal states was little different. Innocent III has gone down in history as the real founder of the papal states, and there is little doubt that the central object of his policy was to ensure the papacy's independence for all time by establishing a substantial territorial state in central Italy under direct papal rule. In this way, he evidently thought, the papacy could withstand Sicilian pressure in the south and German pressure in the north. But his actual achievement was very limited. Otto of Brunswick, angling for the pope's support, was persuaded in 1209 to recognize the papal title to the lands conferred in the various donations from Pippin to the countess Matilda; but it was another question to make these claims effective in face of the resistance of the Italian communes. Here Innocent was at best half successful. The territories were organized, on paper, into four provinces, each under a rector; but in the end the only way the pope could make even his nominal overlordship effective was by handing over central Italy as a fief to marquis Azzo VI of Este, who had the military power to ensure respect for his suzerainty. The establishment of an effective direct government was beyond Innocent's means; and the papal states, far from assuring the papacy's independence, were during the two succeeding centuries more often to prove a millstone round its neck.

The truth is that the administrative machinery at the pope's disposal was inadequate for Innocent III's ambitious policies. It is sometimes said that the papal administration served as a model for the rising monarchies of western Europe, but in sheer efficiency the papacy lagged far behind the feudal states. 'Bureaucracy', in Cheney's words, 'had not developed far enough to meet the needs of government.' When Innocent became pope in 1198 the machine was clogged with petty business and working badly, and the reforms instituted by Gregory VIII and Clement III – even if they were put into operation, which is doubtful – were on too minor a scale to remedy the evil. There is no doubt that Innocent III made a real effort to raise the standards of the curia, and in particular to reform the chancery. He introduced a fixed scale of fees to combat corruption; he organized the *scriptores* as a college; he established the *audientia litterarum contradictarum* as a controlling office for letters of justice; he regulated the position of the proctors; and one of his first acts was to throw out the money-changers who had set up business in a passage near the palace kitchen and sack the majority of the porters and janitors, who held out their palms for money before letting anyone enter the pope's presence. These were all improvements, but on a minor scale, and it would be a mistake to exaggerate their effects. They did not touch the root cause of the trouble – namely, that even Innocent III could not break with the practices of the twelfth century and institute a salaried bureaucracy. He simply lacked the necessary financial resources; and for this reason alone it is an exaggeration to speak, as Poole does, 'of the exactness and perfection with which his chancery was regulated'.

These reservations are not intended to disparage a great pope, but simply to place his pontificate in perspective and indicate the limitations under which he worked. Inevitably, these limitations affected Innocent III's political activities as well. Just as Alexander III's ability to withstand Frederick I was due in large measure to the military power of the Lombard communes, so it is fair to say that Innocent III's successes largely depended on his allies; and too often these allies, like those who supported Gregory VII, were pursuing objects of their own which accorded ill with the pope's aims. The clearest examples of this are the notorious Albigensian crusade, which, to the pope's distress, quickly turned into a war of conquest, and the Fourth Crusade, diverted, once again contrary to Innocent's intention, into an onslaught on the Greek empire of Constantinople. It was the party conflicts in Germany which enabled Innocent to intervene in the imperial question; but when the German parties got together in 1208, he had to back down, and it was only the accident of Philip of Swabia's death which saved him. And in England, laid under interdict in 1208, king John held out against the pope's fulminations until 1213, when gathering baronial discontent and the threat of French invasion forced him to climb down. What is significant, in all these political dealings, is the pope's failure to secure assent to his political conceptions. His interpretation of the relations of empire and papacy was repudiated in Germany, while his interference in England had the paradoxical result of stimulating the growth of national sentiment in the English church. 'There can', says Cheney, 'have been few matters of ecclesiastical politics on which Innocent III's views were shared by any considerable body of English clergy.'

No one would deny the importance of Innocent III's pontificate in the formulation of the theory of papal monarchy. His incisive legal mind set out the papal position with exemplary clarity, and his decretals are famous for their sweeping logic. But in practice he achieved far less than he set out to do, and this discrepancy between theory and practice became a decisive factor under his successors in the thirteenth century, who overstrained themselves in trying to close the gap. If we look back over the history of the papacy from 1122 to 1216, we shall find it hard to disagree with the verdict of the Catholic historian, Albert Dufourcq, when he writes that the results of the effort to build an effective organization of papal government were 'indecisive'. And if we cast our eye further back, and survey the road travelled by the papacy since the reform movement reached Rome under Leo IX, our conclusion will be similar. The progress it had made was immense; the position of the pope in the church was entirely altered; something we have every right to call a papal monarchy was in existence. But the foundations of the papal monarchy were far weaker than is apparent at first glance. Much which looks like planned expansion was, in reality, a surrender to outside pressures, and the administrative apparatus developed to cope with these pressures was little more than a series of hasty, half-thought-out expedients. What was missing, in Dufourcq's words, was 'a man of genius, capable of seeing, willing and compelling'.

The result, by the time of Innocent III's death, was a series of unsolved problems, which were accentuated by his use of his power for political ends. The genuine fervour which had possessed reforming circles at the turn of the eleventh and twelfth centuries, had given way to a preoccupation with organization. The desire among reformers like Humbert, Damian and Hildebrand to shake the church free in order to enable it to pursue its spiritual mission had degenerated into the pursuit of independence for its own sake, generally interpreted in terms of a sovereign papal state. In theory, the church was still conceived of, in Hugh of St Victor's words, as 'the multitude of the Faithful, the whole community of Christians'. In fact, the development of the papal monarchy, with its centre in the curia, had in practice substituted for the church in the wider sense a narrower hierarchical church, the clerical order in its ascending ranks, jealous of its privileges and insistent on its rights; and the ideal and the privileged institution confronted one another at an ever-widening distance. These were the dichotomies which the self-confident advance of the papacy had created. By 1216 the critical moment was drawing near when they would have to be faced – or rather, when (as we shall see) the papacy, by refusing to face them, virtually sealed its own fate.

49, 50 Mosaic representations of the Fourth Crusade (1204)

IV THE PAPAL MONARCHY

THE CRISIS OF THE MEDIEVAL PAPACY

The conventional, and certainly the most convenient, point for a break in the history of the medieval papacy is the pontificate of Innocent IV (1243–54). If the pontificate of Innocent III marked the culmination of the movement for strengthening papal authority which began with Leo IX, it was the pontificate of Innocent IV that saw the start of the long decline which led to the 'Babylonish captivity' at Avignon and the Great Schism.

For this abrupt change many historians have held Innocent IV personally responsible. 'He took the church at her highest and best,' writes A. L. Smith, 'and in eleven years destroyed half her power for good, and launched her irretrievably upon a downward course.' Above all, Innocent IV has been accused of prostituting the power of the papacy for political ends, of using up the capital accumulated by his predecessors in the interests of his political conflict with the emperor Frederick II. It is no doubt easy to exaggerate the contrast between Innocent III and Innocent IV; in their attempt to fix the exact turning-point in the fortunes of the medieval papacy historians may well have exaggerated the achievement of the former and underestimated the elements of continuity. Nevertheless, the fact remains that, from the middle years of the thirteenth century, the papacy was involved at the highest level in European politics: not – as Innocent III had striven to be – as a disinterested arbiter, but as an interested party. It had its own clear-cut political objectives – particularly in Italy and Sicily – which involved it with the rulers of Europe: Innocent IV with Frederick II, Martin IV with Peter the Great of Aragon, Boniface VIII with Philip the Fair. Already under Clement IV (1265–68), a Frenchman who had risen in the service of the Capetian dynasty, the papacy became a tool in the hands of the ambitious Charles of Anjou. But if the most obvious aspect of the situation was the way the church became embroiled in international politics and diplomatic manoeuvres, the repercussions went much deeper. Ultimately, they struck at the very heart of the 'papal monarchy' and changed the whole position of the church in society; and it was these changes, rather than the more superficial political incidents, which counted in the long run.

51 Papal majesty: statue of St Peter in the pontiff's robes and regalia ▶

If we try to summarize the situation of the church at the close of Innocent IV's pontificate in 1254 – or, more broadly, during the long Interregnum between 1250 and 1273, when Innocent IV's successors, particularly Urban IV, were seeking to use the confusion in the empire following Frederick II's death to build up their position in Italy – the central fact is that, after a century and a half of centralization, the 'papal monarchy' had finally been constituted. This may, at first glance, seem an unusually late date at which to place the completion of the transformation of church government. Had not Gregory VII already asserted a distinctly monarchical view of his position at the head of the church? But it was one thing to establish the theoretical foundations of papal monarchy – the origins of which lay far back in the interpretation placed on the primacy of Peter – and another to make it a practical reality. This, as we have seen, was the work of the century and a half preceding the Interregnum; and it was only after the papacy had created the institutions through which to make its authority effective that it was in a position to exercise the judicial, legislative, financial and administrative powers it had gradually accumulated.

The emergence of the pope's legislative power was marked by the promulgation of a new law-book, the 'Decretals', by pope Gregory IX in 1234. Earlier collections, from Gratian's *Decretum* onwards, had been essentially private compilations, but this was an official codification issued under the pope's authority. The pope's judicial supremacy was ensured by the growth of appeals to Rome, and still more by the transfer of cases to Rome in the first instance. This was a longer and more gradual process, which had been gathering pace throughout the twelfth century. When it was consolidated, around the beginning of the thirteenth century, the pope became (in a famous phrase) 'the universal ordinary'; that is to say, his courts were not merely the supreme, but in many cases the ordinary tribunal, hearing causes in the first instance from all parts of Christendom. Even so, there was, to begin with, no properly constituted judiciary. During the first half of the thirteenth century, it was still the practice to delegate cases to *ad hoc* commissions, and it was not until the pontificate of pope Urban IV (1261–64) that a separate court, later known as the *Rota Romana*, was set up to deal with the growing business.

More fundamentally important as a source of papal power and authority was the development of its financial resources. Even after the emergence of the papal *camera* in the early years of the twelfth century, these had remained fairly rudimentary. Papal income at an earlier period had been derived from its landed estates, over which its control was far from secure, and from

120

52 Detail from the 'Decretals' of Gregory IX; from an early fourteenth-century English manuscript ▶

various other minor sources – Peter's Pence, procurations, annual tributes (*census*) from monasteries under papal protection, and the like – which were of limited value, since they were fixed payments which could not be expanded to meet growing needs. The turning-point came with the introduction of an income tax on the clergy. This was introduced in aid of the crusades, but was later put to any and every use. Furthermore, it could be levied at various rates; and though the assessment was standardized by Nicholas IV in 1291, in principle at least it related to real income and grew with it. The first income tax, a fortieth, was levied for the crusade by Innocent III in 1199. The rate was stepped up in 1215, and already in 1228 a tenth was raised to finance the war against Frederick II. Thereafter the impost soon became a general tax, which provided a regular and substantial income, levied on the pope's own authority. Already by the time of Innocent IV the papacy, ahead of most secular rulers, was exercising a well-established power of taxation.

Of all the different facets of papal sovereignty, however, none was more important practically than the control over ecclesiastical benefices, great and small, from archbishoprics and bishoprics down to village churches, by means of papal provisions and papal reservations. Provisions and reservations were closely, and increasingly, tied in with the fiscal system. The first

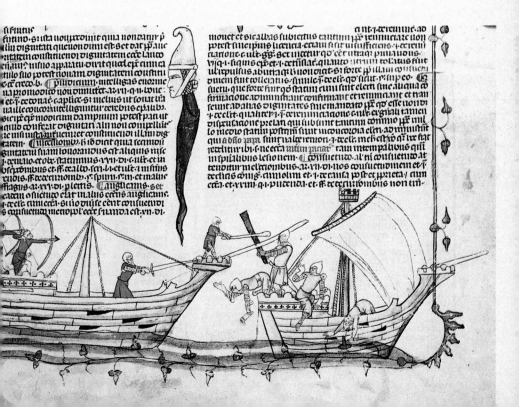

general reservation of bishoprics and major benefices occurred under Innocent IV; it was frequently renewed, for example by Honorius IV in the case of Sicily and by Boniface VIII in the case of France; and finally in 1305 pope Clement V made it a fixed rule that the disposal of all patriarchates, archbishoprics and bishoprics should be reserved to the holy see. In the case of minor benefices (canonries, parish churches, etc.) the first general reservation came under Clement IV in 1265, when the pope reserved for his own disposition all benefices which became vacant through the death of the incumbent at the papal curia. This placed one whole category of benefices in the pope's hands; and although the number involved at first was small, the theory of reservation, once formulated, was capable of rapid expansion by the addition of new classes of benefices to those of which the pope alone could dispose. Boniface VIII and, in the fourteenth century, Clement V and John XXII added new types of 'reserved' benefices; and the whole system of reservations was finally codified by pope Benedict XII in the constitution *Ad regimen* of 1335.

Four points stand out in regard to the developments thus briefly summarized. First, the pope's power as head of the church is essentially unlimited, at least in theory. He has what is called the 'plenitude of power', and the ecclesiastical lawyers say that 'all churches and all the possessions of the churches are in the pope's power'. There are no constitutional checks upon him, no bodies or institutions empowered to exercise control, as the feudal councils did in the secular monarchies, particularly as by now the great synods or councils of the church have been brought under the pope's control. Secondly, the exercise of the pope's powers in all spheres – legal, judicial, financial and in the control of ecclesiastical appointments – requires a very considerable central bureaucracy; in other words, the personnel of the papal curia is growing rapidly, and already showing signs of becoming top-heavy. The keynote of the new system is centralization; the church has become a centralized institution. Thirdly (and springing from this), the spirit of church government is legal; the pope himself is immersed in practical business; the activities of the papal curia are governed by canon law; and the religious functions of the papacy are tending to fall into the background. Already around the middle of the twelfth century St Bernard of Clairvaux had complained of this; and thereafter complaints never ceased. Fourthly, the political factor loomed large, and may even be described as the driving force. Many of the steps through which the popes assumed direct control over the church were dictated by political objectives; for example, Innocent IV's reservation of German bishoprics during the struggle with

53, 54 Philip the Fair and pope Boniface VIII

Frederick II, or Boniface VIII's parallel reservation of French bishoprics during the struggle with Philip the Fair. But over and above this the political activity of the papacy was the main reason for its never satiated need for money. The accounts of the *camera apostolica*, the papal treasury, show that pope John XXII, in the early fourteenth century, spent 63 per cent of his resources on war.

Thus political requirements forced forward centralization and the exploitation of ecclesiastical resources by the papacy. If the papacy had kept aloof from dubious political adventures, it would almost certainly have been well enough off; but its political activities drove it to ever new expedients, which caused indignation and brought it into disrepute. Financial disorder is the mark of papal government as the thirteenth century draws to a close. Living from hand to mouth, nearly always in debt, the holy see gets caught up in a series of expedients, and goes on from expedient to expedient, overburdened with work, heavily in debt, immersed in petty secular transactions, as well as in European politics, until with Boniface VIII it is faced by moral and material bankruptcy.

123

Centralization affected not only the papacy itself but the whole church. In its early stages, perhaps until the end of the twelfth century, it may fairly be argued that centralization was necessary and beneficial. The local prelates were apt to be under royal control or swayed by local and aristocratic influences. Papal control was necessary to give a lead in reform. The trouble was that at no time did the popes stop to ask themselves how far they should go in controlling the bishops and the churches of Europe; no pope tried to draw a line between necessary centralization, which was beneficial, and centralization for its own sake, which was detrimental. They accepted appeals, for example, from all over Christendom, without considering that this mass of judicial business must (as St Bernard had pointed out) divert the pope from his primary religious functions. They accepted them also without due regard to the actual material cost of the growing bureaucracy. But above all else they took away functions and powers from the episcopacy without ever considering the consequences. Centralization was one thing in theory; but in practice it was virtually impossible, in the conditions of the time, for the pope in Rome or Avignon to carry out effectively the detail of church government in every province and diocese of Christendom. The task was too big, the areas to be covered too large.

On the other hand, the effect of the growing papal centralization was to break down the authority of the bishops over their dioceses, and to take away from them one function and necessary power after the other, from control over preachers to the filling of benefices. The result was confusion. Just as there was rarely a balanced budget, so also there was never any clear repartition of duties and functions within the hierarchy. A subordinate could always appeal to Rome against his bishop; a cause which concerned an archbishop would be committed by the pope to some of his suffragans. Thus the papal system, as the prelates complained, subverted the natural order of the church. Because all roads led to Rome no initiative remained with the local prelates, and the diocese – formerly the basic unit of church

◀ 55 The pope in council with clerical and secular councillors; miniature from a late fourteenth-century manuscript .

56 Boniface VIII with the college of cardinals; from a fourteenth-century Bolognese manuscript

government – became an empty shell. Constantly harried by the Roman curia, deprived of initiative, weakened in the face of their subordinates, the bishops became apathetic, lost heart or turned their energies in other directions. The consequence was already visible at the time of the Fourth Lateran Council of 1215, when Innocent III tried to inaugurate a period of reform. The response was negligible. Although some bishops sincerely tried to enforce the reforming decrees, episcopal power was no longer strong enough to become a vehicle of reform, while the pope could only lead and not direct the execution of the decrees in detail. The result was that the necessary reforms were not carried out; and for that result, without doubt, extreme and ill-calculated centralization was primarily responsible.

The other obvious result was that the spiritual life of the dioceses suffered. In that respect, of course, no easy judgment is possible. Under a materialistic or self-seeking bishop, who used livings to promote his friends or relatives, the situation would have been bad also. But it is noticeable and significant that it was the good and genuinely reformatory bishops, like bishop Grosseteste of Lincoln, who complained. Even if the pope's intentions were good – and too often this was not the case – it is obvious that he could not know the requirements of a parish in, say, Lancashire or Donegal as the bishop could. In filling livings by provision he could at best use formal tests of suitability, such as literacy. In actual fact, many papal appointees were absentees and pluralists, because there was a great temptation for the papacy to use its control over ecclesiastical benefices to provide for the bureaucracy of the curia, from the cardinals down to clerks and porters. The complaints of chroniclers like Matthew Paris in England – who said that Innocent IV gave English benefices to the value of 70,000 marks a year to foreigners – were doubtless exaggerated; but there is no doubt that the evil was serious, and did not diminish with time.

In the fourteenth century, when the papacy was at Avignon, there was a strong current of feeling both in England and in Germany that the papacy, by taxation and by disposal of benefices, was taking money out of the country for the benefit of the enemy, France. Almost inevitably, this promoted anti-papal sentiment and anti-papal agitation. But the deficiencies, moral and other, of the clergy, which in part at least were due to the centralization of church institutions, also promoted a new current of anti-clericalism. This anti-clericalism, or anti-sacerdotalism, had its roots in the whole position which the clergy had assumed as a result of the Investiture contest: in particular, in the separation between spiritual and secular, and therefore between clergy and laity, which it was the purpose of the struggle

57 The Fourth Lateran Council (1215); a drawing in the chronicle of Matthew Paris

to enforce. As a result the laity were shut out from a positive part in church affairs; they were the passive element, whereas the active role was increasingly concentrated in the hands of the clergy, who were the mediators between the people and God, and whose control of the sacraments gave them a privileged position. Step by step, active lay participation was diminished. Under Alexander III, for example, the rights of patrons were whittled away, until they became a mere formality; and at the third Lateran council in 1179 the election of the bishop, which a century earlier had been the joint concern of clergy and people, was vested exclusively in the hands of the cathedral chapters.

Already in the twelfth century these changes produced a reaction, which later took many different forms, but which thereafter never died down. As conditions became more settled and more prosperous, particularly in the towns, there was a growing tendency among the laity, especially the wealthy merchant classes, to ponder upon religious truth, which soon led to the view that all men are called upon to play an equal part in religious activity. This attitude, anti-sacerdotal in essence, was strengthened by observation of the growing wealth and materialism of the clergy, the hunt for

127

fat livings, the accumulation of benefices, and so on. In reaction, the ideal of Christian poverty was set up, and of an apostolic life of wandering and preaching; for preaching, before the thirteenth century, still played little part in the formal activities of the church, which centred round the liturgy and the sacraments. The result of these movements was a growing scepticism about the validity of the ecclesiastical order, which seemed to have departed far from apostolic poverty. The elaborate legal and institutional system appeared to have little direct relation with the teachings of the Gospels, which more and more were set up as the only valid standard of Christian life. The upshot was a reaction against the hierarchy, which quickly took shape in the twelfth century on the heels of the new centralization, and was perhaps its inevitable sequel. The papal curia had the atmosphere of a law-court or business-office; inevitably the best elements turned elsewhere for spiritual leadership. But precisely because it was the best and most serious and religious-minded people who were alienated, the church itself, the official hierarchy, tended to become more and more a vested interest of placemen, wealthy benefice-hunters, successful lawyers practising in the church courts, royal clerks preferred through royal influence. Evidently, it was not a healthy development.

The first sign of this reaction was the extraordinary growth, in the twelfth century, of heresies. Much has been written about the doctrines propounded by these heretical movements, particularly the Cathars. But the real cause of the heretical movements was not doctrinal difference, but protest against a secularized church. It is true that some reformatory circles, particularly in Lombardy and southern France, were affected by Manicheism, and by other dualistic philosophies coming from the east; and the church, in order to combat them, put all the emphasis in its polemics on the dualistic doctrines and their alleged moral consequences. But in reality it was not the speculative problems, but the question of the form of religious life and of the organization of the church that was at the root of the matter. The Poor Men of Lyons, for example, or the Waldensians preached a primitive religion, akin to that of the apostles; they stood for spiritual values, poverty, preaching, salvation, against the throttling incubus of the rigid and largely secularized hierarchy. Against these movements, the church at first resorted to repression, but with little effect; the social forces behind them were too strong to be easily stamped out. In fact, it was only when the church made the great decision to enlist the same forces on its side – when, in other words, it opened a place for 'popular religion' within the church – that it had some measure of success in combating, though only

58, 59 St Dominic (left) and St Francis; two thirteenth-century representations

through repression and the inquisition, the popular religious movements which remained outside.

This enlistment of popular elements – which was a real revolution, giving a new character to the church – was achieved, as is well known, by the recognition given to the mendicant orders, the Dominicans and the Franciscans. The former were commissioned, around 1206, to combat the heretics with their own weapon of wandering preaching. The origins of the Franciscans, on the other hand, were very similar to those of earlier heretical movements, such as the Poor Men of Lyons, and it was only by a hair's breadth – and by good luck and deep insight – that they also escaped condemnation as heretics. The insight came from pope Innocent III who – aware of the failure of the earlier repressive methods to combat the popular movements effectively – forced through the recognition of St Francis against the opposition of the prelates and of the monastic orders, particularly of the Cistercians (by now a vested interest fighting for their rights), at the Fourth Lateran Council in 1215. It may truly be said that his action in opening up a place in the church for the popular movements – on rigorous conditions, including absolute obedience to the holy see – was the greatest

129

merit of a great pope. It saved the church from petrifaction in a rigid hierarchy; it made possible its adaptation to the requirements of a new social environment – namely, the rising towns with their urban proletariat – which the old parochial organization, adapted primarily to the needs of the countryside, scarcely touched; it allowed room for new, lively spirits of deep religious feeling, which earlier policy had driven out of the church. But like all great decisions of the sort, it marked both an end and a beginning; it answered one series of questions but opened up another. And it is with the consequences of Innocent III's policy, rather than his immediate achievement, that we are here concerned.

A full consideration would require a fairly detailed examination of the history of the mendicant orders in the thirteenth century. All that it is necessary to say is that, in binding them closely to the papacy and making them an instrument of papal policy, the pope inevitably altered their character, in particular that of the followers of St Francis. This was not so much the work of Innocent III or of his immediate successor, Honorius III, as of Gregory IX, who as cardinal Ugolino of Ostia had been St Francis' friend and admirer and protector since 1217. There was nothing sinister about pope Gregory IX's attitude or policy. He had a genuine and deep admiration for Francis, and regarded his followers as the healthiest element in the church. But precisely because of this, he wanted to enlist them actively as agents of reform. By the time of Gregory IX's accession in 1227 the ineffectiveness of the reforming decrees of 1215, which Innocent III had tried to promulgate through the episcopacy, was evident; and it almost seems as if the new pope despaired of the secular clergy, and saw in the Mendicants the only hope of infusing the church with an effective spirit of religious and reforming fervour. Wholehearted support of the friars, Gregory apparently believed, offered the most immediate promise of betterment and success. Paradoxically, however, his policy of reliance upon the friars added to, rather than solved, the problems within the church.

First of all, it caused dissension within the Franciscan order, a split between the two wings, the Conventuals and the Spirituals. The organization of what in origin had been a free movement into a religious order with a fixed rule, inevitably changed the spirit of the Franciscans. Whether it was a departure from St Francis' own intentions has been hotly debated, and the arguments need not detain us. Perhaps with the passage of time the adoption of a monastic type of organization was inevitable, and without it the movement would have collapsed; nevertheless the transformation was resisted. On the one side, the majority easily took their place among the existing orders and, devoting themselves to preaching, took up the study of theology in order to preach sound doctrine. By the middle of the thirteenth century Dominicans and Franciscans were firmly ensconced in the universities, and were already the leading lights in the intellectual sphere. They had fixed houses and, as study needed an income, were amassing revenues. The other wing saw in this a betrayal of St Francis' aims, and demanded strict poverty (i.e., living on alms and begging) and dissolution of the houses. The struggle went on through the thirteenth century, and the cleavage was abrupt. But the Spirituals, or Fraticelli, although a minority, held out, and because of their idealism won widespread support, both among the people and among princes, which made them a major force. They appealed to the spirituality of the age, and when, from about the middle of the thirteenth century, their doctrine of apostolic poverty was fused with other ideas stemming from Joachim of Fiore, they came to enjoy very extensive influence.

Joachim, a Cistercian who found in the Cistercianism of his day little spiritual satisfaction, had founded a congregation of his own at the monastery of San Giovanni di Fiore in Calabria, marked by asceticism and mysticism. Joachim, who died in 1202, was no heretic, nor even a revolutionary, though later on his doctrines were condemned. He was a friend of the popes of his time, Lucius III and Urban III; but his speculative thought, based on a wide knowledge of the Bible and on the ancient lore of numbers, was both a solvent and a response to the need of the time for a more spiritual and less dialectical approach to religion. As an ascetic, he had great disdain for the world, most of all for theologians, who presumed to rationalize the faith, and for the secular clergy, whose lives were anything but ascetic and no reflection of the example of the apostles. Here, in the apostolic ideal and the desire for a return to the apostolic age, is the link between Joachim and the Spiritual Franciscans, who began in the second half of the thirteenth century to take up, develop and propagate his teachings.

Joachim's doctrines gave the cry for apostolic poverty a realistic basis which hitherto it had lacked. According to Joachim there were three ages, one corresponding to the Old Testament, the second to the New Testament; the third, which was still to come, would be a new age of the Holy Spirit, which would supersede the decadent church. Thus the church, as it was, represented not a finality, but merely a stage which would pass; and the fundamental importance of Joachim's cosmology was that it shattered the church's pretensions to represent the Kingdom of God on earth. But there was still the practical question: when would the second age pass?

131

The Spiritual Franciscans had an answer. St Francis himself represented the dawn of the new era. The church, borne down by wealth and corruption, would collapse in 1260.

It is hard to exaggerate the effects of this visionary scheme. Even when the new era failed to arrive in 1260, prophecies of the end of the age and the beginning of a new one continued to proliferate. They were in the air, reported by chroniclers, throughout the latter part of the thirteenth and the beginning of the fourteenth century. And the visionaries were taken up by statesmen of all types, including Charles of Anjou and his son's opponent, the Aragonese ruler of Sicily, Frederick, partly out of genuine conviction, partly as a stick with which to beat the hierarchy. It was the Spiritual Franciscans who provided support for Louis of Bavaria against pope John XXII; and though ultimately they were crushed by the inquisition, tortured out of existence, they lit a flame which was not extinguished. The great mystical tradition, with its implied and open criticism of the legalistic church and the hierarchy, stems from Joachim of Fiore and St Francis, and

60, 61 Page from a late thirteenth-century manuscript of Joachim of Fiore's *I tre regni e la Trinità* (far left); the drawing depicts the Holy Trinity. Left, a marginal drawing of a Franciscan and Dominican friar, from a mid fourteenth-century English treatise on ecclesiastical poverty, including its abuse by friars. (The Franciscan has a devil on his back.)

62 *The Dream of Innocent III*. This fresco from Giotto's St Francis cycle at Assisi shows the saint preserving the Lateran basilica

never dies until the Reformation. In fact, it does not die then either, but goes over into the Protestant sects. It was a fundamental fact in the history of the fourteenth, fifteenth and sixteenth centuries, because the claim to an active religious life for all the faithful, a direct and mystical communion with God, which any man through God's grace might enjoy, was essentially irreconcilable – even when its propounders remained within the church and escaped branding as heretics – with the church's claim that the only road to salvation was through the sacraments administered by a duly authorized clergy.

The attack on the Spiritual Franciscans, brought to a conclusion by pope John XXII in the fourteenth century but initiated far earlier, was one of the factors most effective in undermining respect for the papacy; for the genuine spirituality of the friars was beyond all dispute, and it seemed wicked for a pope living in luxury in his palace in Avignon to condemn them for maintaining the doctrine of apostolic poverty. Wicked, self-interested, and worldly. On the other hand, the reliance placed by the papacy, from the time of Gregory IX, on the more orthodox friars embroiled the papacy with the prelates. To allow the Mendicants to operate more fully, they were given privileges and exemptions. They were allowed to preach, for example, without the bishop's licence; they were allowed to bury those who wished to be associated with them in their own churchyards, and to collect the mortuary fees to the detriment of the parish clergy. These privileges were probably necessary in face of the hostility of the secular clergy and bishops. But as the thirteenth century proceeded, and privilege was piled on privilege, the result was to break down the authority of the bishop and the unity of the diocese. In this way a conflict, often not very dignified or disinterested on either side, arose between the prelates and the friars; and the papacy was quickly involved, because it was the pope's privileges which had raised the friars up.

Inevitably, therefore, criticism turned against the papacy itself, and the church became a body divided. This was important when conflict arose between church and state, between king and pope – for example, between Philip the Fair and Boniface VIII – because it meant that there was always one section, at least, of the clergy which supported the royal standpoint. The pope, they said, by his privileges and exemptions, was upsetting the divinely-appointed order of the church; and gradually they came to look to the monarchy to defend this order, if need be, against the pope himself. Here, quite early, was the beginning of the royal claim to intervene – as a king ruling by God's grace – in the affairs of the church of his land when, in his view, they stood in need of betterment, which was to become so important at the time of the Reformation.

These developments are graphically illustrated by the history of the great councils of the church: the Fourth Lateran Council of 1215, the First Council of Lyons in 1245, the Second Council of Lyons in 1274, and the Council of Vienne in 1311. The differences of tone and atmosphere between these councils mark with extraordinary clarity the changing attitude to the church, to reform and to the papacy.

In 1215 the papacy was at the centre; it was the pope, Innocent III, who drew up the programme of reform, to be put into effect by the bishops, and it was to the papacy that people looked, in the old spirit, to reform the church. Leadership came from the pope, and reform was the essential purpose of the synod. Innocent's objectives were, on the one hand, to combat heresy and paganism, and, on the other hand, to eradicate the abuses through which, if they were not remedied, heresy was bound to flourish; and the method used, or proposed, was centralization and central control. By 1245, the objects had changed. The sins of the clergy were still one of the items on the agenda; but now political issues were predominant – the peril of the Latin empire of Constantinople, the powerlessness of the Christians in the Holy Land, the incursions of Mongols and Tartars into eastern Europe, and above all else the conflict with Frederick II.

In fact, the conflict with Frederick II was the real reason for the summoning of the council of 1245 by Innocent IV; it was an attempt, only partly successful, to mobilize Christian opinion against the emperor. And it is characteristic of the First Council of Lyons that its decrees, so far as they concerned internal church affairs, were 'entirely confined to technical questions of law and procedure'. This shows how far, in only a short generation, the legal spirit had increased at the curia. But the most significant thing at the First Council of Lyons was the attack on the whole papal system of government, an attack coming from England but backed up, a couple of years later, by a similar denunciation, the *Gravamina ecclesiæ Gallicanæ* of 1247, from France. If, in other words, it had been a question in 1215 of the reform of the 'members' by the 'head', in 1245 it was realized that the 'head' also was in need of reform. Papal taxation and papal provision to benefices – papal 'extortion', as the critics now no longer hesitated to describe it – were the burden of both the English and the French complaints; but the charge went deeper when St Louis himself intervened, asserting that the pope was doing new things, new and unheard of, *nova et inaudita*, and that this was the root cause of the evil in the church.

This charge of innovation clearly implied the subversion of the old ecclesiastical order, and fell into line with the charge of the Spiritual Franciscans that the church, through papal action, was departing further and further from the example of the apostles and the apostolic precepts. It implied a condemnation of the whole centralized system of church government as an excrescence, which – people would later say – must be removed to get back to the true ecclesiastical order. As yet people did not say this; they failed to draw the logical corollary, still hoped that the pope himself would draw a line and put things right. But the appeal of the English clergy in 1246 to a future general council is significant, particularly as Frederick II, claiming that Innocent IV was not impartial and that the council of 1245 was not representative, had already made the same appeal. It shows that people still thought the ecumenical council was above the pope; that there was a further recourse, a higher tribunal.

In 1274, because Gregory X was a greater man than Innocent IV, with a more profound understanding of the church's needs, reform was far more prominent than it had been in 1245. Partly, without doubt, this was because Innocent IV's own activities, his unhesitating use of the church's resources for political purposes, had made the question of reform far more urgent, and even those among his successors who looked with disfavour on Innocent's policy – Alexander IV, for example – had failed to provide an effective remedy for his abuses. For Gregory X the situation in the east, the reunion of the Latin and Greek churches, and joint action against the Turks, were no doubt the ultimate objects. But he perceived that the dissipation of religious fervour by the political use which Innocent IV and succeeding popes (such as Clement IV) had made of their power, and the consequent disillusion with the papacy, stood in the way of the crusade he desired, and that before action against the Turks was possible reform was necessary to restore a united Christendom. The misuse of crusading tithes for political ends had caused disgust; and the situation between 1250 and 1273 – above all, the part played by the papacy in the destruction of the empire – had produced widespread pessimism. Instead of zeal and belief in the papacy, there was general criticism. To meet this criticism Gregory, before the council, sent round a circular asking for reports on conditions to serve as a basis for reform; and in fact reports were received – and are still extant – from the General of the Dominicans, Humbert of Romans, from the Franciscans, and from one of the bishops, Bruno of Olmütz.

These reports cast a revealing light on the state of western Christendom at the beginning of the last quarter of the thirteenth century; in particular, they reveal the disorder introduced into the church by papal support for the Mendicants against the secular clergy, and the bitter feeling aroused thereby, as well as the weakening of the position of the parish priests towards the laity resulting from the preference given to the friars. Nor is there any hesitation in attacking the abuses of the Roman curia. But, in the last analysis,

63, 64 Illustrations to Dante's *Divine Comedy* from an early fifteenth-century Sienese manuscript. Below (*Inferno*, canto 19), Virgil and Dante enter from the left and Dante speaks to pope Nicholas III, a notorious simoniac who is buried head downwards. Bottom (*Purgatory*, canto 19), Dante and Virgil talk with the nude pope Hadrian among the avaricious and the prodigal

there is a curious hesitancy about all these writings. It is seen that the papacy is responsible for many of the evils in the church; but at the same time there seems to be no hope of betterment except through the pope. In effect, the papacy is asked to reform itself.

In this sense the council of 1274 represents, we may say, a halfway house. The evils at the centre are recognized, but the papacy is not attacked. When we come to the council of Vienne in 1311 this is no longer the case. This was, in intention at least, a council similar in character to that of 1245; that is to say, it was summoned essentially for political reasons. Its main practical task, under pressure from Philip the Fair, was to dissolve the Order of Templars, whose goods and chattels the French king coveted. Its second main object, by surrender over the Templars, was to ward off the attack on the memory of Boniface VIII, whom the French wished to condemn post-humously as a heretic. All in all, it was not an edifying assembly. But Clement V, memorable of Gregory X's example, also circulated before-hand a memorandum asking for proposals for reform; and in this way he opened the door for an attack on the papacy, such as no other council had made. Two bishops at least, William Lemaire of Angers and William Durand of Mende, made frontal attacks on the whole system, and there is evidence of other criticism from the body of the council.

Durand's attack was so fierce that he was arrested and kept in prison for seven years and more, in spite of protests from the French king. Now it was said, quite plainly and openly, that if there were to be reform, it must start with the 'head', the Roman curia, and that if there were no reform the blame would lie squarely with the pope and the cardinals and the synod. The first thing was to put an end to the sale of offices and dispensations, from which the curia lived. The taxes the papacy levied from those to whom it granted benefices, *servitia* and annates, were no better than simony. And so on. But Durand went further, maintaining that the pope was bring-ing confusion into the whole ecclesiastical order, by depriving the prelates of their rights – namely to hear suits arising in their dioceses, and to provide for their own clergy. Things had reached such a pass, he added, that the clerks of the papal chancery had precedence over archbishops. It was the pope's duty to respect the ancient law of the church, and to change it only with the consent of the general council, which should meet every ten years. The pope's primacy was not denied, but it was time for it to be defined; it should be stated exactly to what it extended, both in the spiritual and in the temporal spheres. In short, what Durand demanded was the abolition of the papal *plenitudo potestatis*, of the unlimited powers, which had grown up in

138

the course of the previous century, and a return to the old constitution, with a restoration of the independent authority of bishops and of synods.

Here is the ideal of an ecclesiastical constitution on the basis of episcopacy and council, which was to become a force at the beginning of the fifteenth century. But Durand was before his time, and, as has already been noted, he was imprisoned and his teachings were suppressed. If he could propound such ideas publicly in the council, it was because of the struggle between Philip the Fair and Boniface VIII, during which royal propagandists and pamphleteers – such as John of Paris – had developed similar attacks on the papal primacy from the point of view of the secular power, setting limits on papal pretensions by announcing the independent and equal authority of the king. But it was another thing when criticism and opposition occurred within the church; for this implied a clerical opposition, a demand not for the independence of the state, but for a balanced constitution for the ecclesiastical order. Durand misfired, however, first and foremost, because he did not have the backing of the secular power. After 1303 the conflict of Philip the Fair with the Roman church had been settled. The French king had learnt that more was to be gained by pressure on the pope, by wringing concessions from him, and by a tacit agreement between the two powers to despoil the church. For this there were already many precedents, particularly in taxation, where the kings only allowed the papal tax collectors to operate in their lands on condition that the monarchy participated in the proceeds. Already in the thirteenth century the kings of France and England and Spain were securing the lion's share of papal taxes on the clergy; already they were using the papal powers of provision to benefices to get their candidates – royal servants and officials – placed in canonries and bishoprics by papal action at the cost of the ordinary collator. What was the point of upsetting this happy compromise by a quarrel with the pope? Co-operation was better than conflict, and radical attacks on the papal position were simply held in reserve as a means of putting pressure on the pope, if he was not prepared to give the ruler as much as he desired.

Throughout the Avignonese period from 1309 to 1376 this was the usual situation. The frontal attack which Philip the Fair had initiated in the days of Boniface VIII was in abeyance. Nevertheless the criticism at the council of Vienne in 1311 – though it was the last of its sort for upward of three generations – frightened the papacy. It is significant that after 1311 no new general council of the church was summoned for over a century; and when the next general council – the sixteenth – met at Constance in 1414 the situation was very different. For in fact none of the reform projects, neither

those of 1274 nor those of 1311, came to anything; and after 1311, for the
very lack of a constitutional means of airing grievances and seeking redress,
the abuses of which William Lemaire and William Durand had complained, grew apace, furthered by the adverse conditions which faced the
papacy after 1309 at Avignon.

THE BABYLONISH CAPTIVITY

If all attempts at reform came to nothing, it was not, of course, because
there was no realization at the curia of the need for reform. Many of the
popes of the thirteenth century, such as Gregory X, were men of high moral
calibre; and there was always at least a group in the college of cardinals
aware of the needs of the situation. It is remarkable, if one follows the
history of the papacy step by step, how often, after a pontificate filled with
political activity, there is a complete reaction. The common idea of continuity in papal policy, of centralization advancing step by step from pontificate to pontificate, is in many respects misleading. After Innocent IV, for
example, the cardinals elected the pacific Alexander IV, who did not hide
his distaste for the policy of his predecessor, and who took steps, in regard to
the grant of benefices, to undo Innocent's abuses. Similarly, the election of
Gregory X, a deeply religious man, was a reaction by the cardinals against
the pontificate of Clement IV. It was the same in the fourteenth century.
The warlike, fiery, intemperate John XXII was followed by the moderate,
reformatory Benedict XII who tried to make peace with Louis of Bavaria.

In all this, politics and reform were connected; for the idea behind the
election of moderates, ready to compromise over political issues and seek a
political settlement, was to free the church from the strain and expense of
political adventures in order to win a breathing-space during which to concentrate on internal reform. And yet experience showed that there was no
salvation in a change of person, because it was the system that was at fault;
and no pope could bring himself to attack the system – it was too much like
sawing off the branch on which he was sitting. Consequently the mild and
genuinely reformatory popes brought not reform, but troubles and difficulties of a different kind. The most famous occasion of all was the election
of the Calabrian hermit, Peter Morone, a figure in the tradition of Joachim
of Fiore, in 1294. Without doubt this election reflected the intense realization of the need for a total change. It was a triumph of the spiritual element,
and there was a lively belief that Peter, as Celestine V, would restore the
reign of poverty and re-establish Christianity in its pure evangelical form.
What happened, of course, was different. Celestine had no experience of

140

65 The pope at bottom left of this detail from a fourteenth-century fresco
by Andrea di Firenze may be Clement V, first of the Avignonese popes ▶

practical affairs; he could not stand up to pressure; he was unable to cope with the vast machine that church government has become; and after only a few weeks he abdicated. But the disillusion and disappointment arising from this failure made things even worse than before, discouraged all the reformatory elements, and produced a swing of the pendulum. It was no accident that Celestine V was succeeded by Boniface VIII, a lawyer by training, and the most politically-minded pope since Innocent IV. A shrewd, businesslike, dominating pope was required to get the church out of the predicaments in which Celestine, the hermit, had landed it; and reformers were needed to get it out of the predicaments in which the politicians landed it.

There is something infinitely dispiriting in all this – above all else, in the way the genuine and lively religious impulses in the church were frustrated and came to nothing, and each attempt at remedy produced something worse. It was the same in the fourteenth century, after the removal of the curia to Avignon. The popes of Avignon, long besmirched by Protestant propaganda, were an extraordinarily varied collection of men; every type of pope was tried to set the church on its feet again, for by now no one, not even the popes themselves, felt that the position was healthy; but without result. The popes of Avignon started off, of course, from a very different position from their thirteenth-century predecessors. The pontificate of Boniface VIII, too often regarded as a high point of papal pretensions, had in reality been a disaster of the first magnitude for the church, and it was only the English victories in the Hundred Years War in the middle of the fourteenth century – Crécy in 1346 and Poitiers in 1356 – that in some measure gave back to the papacy its freedom of action, by relieving the pressure from France. Even so, it is instructive to follow briefly the succession of pontiffs, and their different attitudes and policies, because a survey shows that, in the end, it was not the persons that mattered, but the system that was at fault.

Clement V (1305–14), the first of the Avignonese popes, suffered throughout his pontificate from the circumstances in which he succeeded to the holy see. He had the spectacle of Boniface VIII always before his eyes; feared always, not without reason, the same fate – not perhaps so much for himself personally, as for the very real danger that the papacy might be 'enslaved' if he provoked France to direct intervention.

Clement's election reflected the conditions arising from the conflict of Philip the Fair and Boniface VIII. Once again, as at so many crises in papal history, the cardinals went outside their own circle, and elected a pope who had not been cardinal, the archbishop of Bordeaux. One main reason was the sharp division in the college between the French and Italian factions, and between the defenders and opponents of Boniface VIII. The upshot of these divisions, and of open French threats of what would happen if a 'Bonifacian' were chosen, was the election of the outsider, Clement. But it also seems probable – though it is a point which has escaped historians – that the choice reflected a genuine attempt to step outside the existing parties. Clement, as archbishop of Bordeaux, was a subject of the king of England; and his election was probably a last effort to secure some sort of independence for the papacy by enlisting English support – as Boniface VIII had tried to do in the last months of his pontificate – and by playing off Edward I against France. If so, it misfired. By 1305 Edward I, who had burnt his fingers in the crisis of 1297–98 and still had the Scottish complication on his hands, had withdrawn into isolation, and refused to be caught up again in European entanglements. He did nothing to help Clement maintain his independence, and step by step between 1305 and 1309 the pope was brought into dependence on France.

After his election, Clement set off by slow stages for Italy, but never got there. When he got to Poitiers in 1308, Philip the Fair occupied the town with French troops, as though he were going to repeat the incident of Anagni. He did the same again at Lyons in 1312, when it seemed that the council might not condemn the Templars, as he demanded. The pressure, on both occasions, was too much for Clement. In 1312 he forced the unwilling council to concur by a threat of excommunication. Perhaps to the end he hoped to escape; but he never did. His support for the German ruler, Henry VII, whom he actually made emperor, was given without doubt in the hope that Henry, by action in Italy, would enable him to return to Rome; he had the idea, like Gregory X before him, of strengthening the German ruler in order to use him as a counterweight to France. But when Henry's Italian campaign was opposed by the new Angevin ruler in Naples, Robert, Clement veered round and withdrew his support in face of combined Franco-Angevin threats.

These negotiations revealed Clement V's essential weakness. He used every stratagem, twisted and turned, intrigued and manœuvred, but in the end against a determined opponent – and both Philip and Robert were determined and unscrupulous – he gave way. As an outsider without a party, he was, of course, in a weak position; but the way to secure a party was determined measures, and here he failed. Instead, he sought to build up a party by conferring cardinals' hats on his relatives; but the sole result was to add still another faction – the Gascons – to the college of cardinals. Of twenty-four cardinals created by Clement, no less than twenty-three were born within the frontiers of modern France, and the Italian element was put in a permanent minority. It was, in Renan's words, 'one of the most abrupt revolutions' in ecclesiastical history.

In addition, because he was cut off from his Italian dominions and from the income from them – Italy was going its own way under local lords – Clement was driven to increased taxation. He it was who introduced annates, i.e., the payment of the first year's revenue by the recipient from every benefice conferred by the pope. And this source of income led, naturally enough, to a rapid increase in papal provisions. In fact, Clement amassed a very considerable sum of money; but owing to his feebleness of character, the greatest profit went to the place-hunters at the curia, to his own family and dependants, which gave him a bad name as a 'simonist'; while his lack of attention to administrative detail led to abuses at the curia itself by the officials, who demanded exorbitant payments for every service. And though he accumulated an estimable treasure, it was not used for the church; about half went to his relatives, and a third was lent to the kings of France and England, with little prospect of repayment. All in all, the pontificate of Clement V – probably a well-intentioned, but certainly a lamentably weak man – can only be described as a decidedly bad start.

His successor, John XXII (1316–34), elected after a long vacancy, was a very different man, and a very different man was needed. John XXII was an organizer, by inclination and by training; he had previously been chancellor of the king of Naples, and that had the incidental advantage that he was acquainted – although by birth a Frenchman from Cahors – with Italian conditions. But John XXII was not only an efficient organizer; he was also a man with the disposition of a ruler, 'vir ardentis ingenii', with determination and will-power, and no inclination to fall into easy compromises; a man of energy, clear-headed and relentless. In addition – and here the contrast between him and Clement V was marked – he was, like most men of his type, a person of simple habits and sober living, with few personal requirements, and disdainful of unnecessary luxury; not a man, in short, to waste the church's resources on high living, when there were more urgent calls on its purse. The more one knows of John XXII, the more one finds to admire in his qualities, and perhaps above all in his many-sidedness. But one also realizes that, in other respects, he lacked the attributes of greatness. He was too inflexible, too logical, too convinced of his own rightness. And though, after Clement V, these qualities were needed,

66 The election of pope John XXII (1316) by the conclave, after a long vacancy ▶

they were not the only qualities needed. Precisely because his was so positive a character, where Clement's had been negative, John XXII provoked an opposition which Clement's more easy-going rule had not aroused. Clement was condemned for simony, for nepotism, for luxury, for waste; John XXII aroused fierce theological and political resistance. And his efficiency in the organization of papal government perhaps did more to bring the papacy into disrepute than Clement's slackness.

John XXII had a perfectly clear political plan, which was to restore the church's independence – by which he meant the papacy's independence – by building up a balance of power: a balance of power in Italy and a balance of power, more generally, in Europe. He stood well with the French king but – particularly in the kingdom of Arles – he opposed French expansion, favouring instead the house of Anjou. In Italy, on the other hand, he opposed the Angevins – or rather he opposed the ambitions of Robert of Naples, whose main object was to prevent a revival of the empire, instead to get himself lodged in Lombardy, and ultimately to rule the whole of Italy as a king. This would have permanently affected the position of the papacy, and John therefore set out to confine Robert – with whom, however, his relations remained good – to the south. He perceived that a

restoration of the position in Germany was necessary, and looked to an alliance with the Habsburgs, hoping indeed to place them in Lombardy as a counterpoise to Robert. Such an equilibrium, he hoped, would enable the papacy to return to Rome and control central Italy, and this would give it an independent position and adequate material resources.

The independence of the papacy, and the return to Italy which was its essential precondition, were thus John XXII's ultimate objects; and he did not shrink from the means – namely, the equipping of a papal army to re-conquer the Italian territories, from Bologna south. Indeed, Bologna rather than Rome was to be the seat of the papal court. This involved the pope in war with the Visconti of Milan; but the essential difficulty lay north of the Alps in Germany, where the Habsburgs had failed to establish their position. In 1314 there had been a double election in Germany, which was divided into pro- and anti-Habsburg parties; and Louis of Bavaria, the leader of the anti-Habsburg party, was successful. It was characteristic of John XXII that he refused to recognize this fact. His motives are not easy to uncover; it is as if, having backed the wrong horse, he was too stubborn to admit his error. Certainly he was aware that Louis entertained ambitions of intervening in Italy, with the support of the Visconti and the Italian Gibelins. But it was equally clear that the Habsburgs, if successful, would not have been disinterested in Lombardy either. In any case, the pope rejected all Louis' overtures – although the latter had every reason to seek a compromise – and finally excommunicated him.

There is no doubt that John XXII's obstinacy inflamed opinion against him. His assertion that the imperial throne was vacant, his claim to admin-ister the empire (i.e., Italy) during the vacancy, his demand to examine and adjudicate upon the election of Louis, were widely regarded as out-rageous, and Louis quickly became the centre of resistance to the pope's pretensions. Thus, the old argument of the days of Philip the Fair and Boniface VIII was revived. Louis, with Gibelin support, went to Rome (1328) and had himself crowned emperor at the hands of representatives of the 'Roman people'. He declared John deposed as a heretic, and a new pope, a Franciscan, Pietro Rainalducci, was set up in his place as Nicholas V. Here the connection between Louis and the clerical opposition of the Spiritual Franciscans, whom John was busy hounding out of existence, becomes clear. But Louis also had at his court a number of philosophers and theoret-icians who took up the cry of Philip the Fair's propagandists, and went even further. Marsilius of Padua did not simply proclaim the independence of the state from the church, but argued that the church was merely an organ of the self-sufficient state. Other anti-papalists at Louis' court were the Frenchman, Jean of Jandun, and the Englishman, William Ockham. The practical effort of their anti-papal theories was not great; on the whole it is fair to say that they served, if anything, to bring Louis into disrepute and to lose him the sympathy which many felt. But when Louis withdrew from the attack to the defensive, and simply asserted his own independent position, support was general in Germany, and even the Habsburgs gave him their backing.

Thus the effect of John's policy was to provoke a national opposition in Germany, and consolidate Louis' position. In Italy his attempt to bring in French and Czech and Austrian troops to help retrieve the position in Lombardy, resulted in a similar Italian national reaction, which took shape in the League of Ferrara (1333). At the time of his death, in 1334, John XXII's imperial and Italian policy was a failure – and probably an unnecessary failure. Never for a moment was there any sign of compromise, or any serious attempt to reach a settlement with Louis. Even the cardinals were outraged, and doubted the pope's wisdom. At the very end, in 1334, the cardinal of Comminges said openly to John: 'Holy Father, believe me, this rigour may be lawful, but it is not expedient.'

The same rigour – perhaps a reaction against the laxity of Clement V – marks John XXII's treatment of the church. Clement V, characteristically, had tried to reconcile the Spiritual Franciscans, to tread a path of compromise and mediation. John XXII never hesitated for one moment; they were condemned, handed over to the inquisition, burnt at the stake. Nor was this a reaction to their attacks on his regiment; it preceded them, and it was the pope who opened hostilities, and pursued them relentlessly. The dogma of apostolic poverty was condemned (1323); Christ, the pope declared, though he may have lived as a poor man, used and respected the rights of property. This was an attack, not only on the Spirituals, but on the central tenet of the whole Franciscan order; and their General did not hesitate to accuse the pope of heresy. The papal pronouncement, precisely because it was so unnecessary and so extreme, caused consternation; it seemed as though the official church were against the Gospels, the papacy corrupted by riches. So far as John XXII personally is concerned, this charge was unjust. His reputation of a stern, strict ruler is on the whole warranted. By his famous constitution *Execrabilis* he forced all holders of pluralities without dispensation to surrender all save the last benefice acquired, and limited dispensations to a total of two benefices. It was certainly a reforming decree, which aroused widespread opposition. But it was also pointed out that all

67 The pope judging heretics; from a late fourteenth-century Bolognese manuscript

benefices vacated in this way were reserved to the pope, and not a few critics maintained that the pope's purpose was not reform, but to increase his revenues.

In fact, although John XXII was not personally lavish, the keynote of his pontificate is contained in the one word: fiscalism. The new tax on benefices introduced by Clement V, the annates, was systematized, methods of collection were perfected. The papal curia, out of hand under Clement, was reorganized; new ordinances of the greatest detail were drawn up for the chancery, the law-courts and other offices, and the payments to the chancery, formerly for work done, were transformed into chancery taxes, graded according to the value to the recipient of the concession made. It was the same with regard to the reservation of benefices: the whole system was reviewed and systematized by the constitution *Ex debito*, but in the process it was made more rigid.

John XXII was a first-class organizer and administrator, able to reduce everything to system; but thereby he only made the centralization more inflexible. He weakened the bishops by dividing up large dioceses. He centralized because it was in his nature to centralize, and because he had supreme confidence in the benefits of his own control. The trouble was that the system he created – by and large, with good intentions – outlasted him,

and was later used by popes whose objects were fiscal pure and simple. In this respect – by completing the centralization of church institutions, and particularly by placing papal finance on a systematic foundation – John XXII's pontificate shaped the future. The constitutions he issued, the so-called *Decretales extravagantes* or 'Extravagants', which he added in a new book to canon law, became from his time the practical basis of ecclesiastical administration; the old law went into desuetude, just as the *Decretum* had been superseded in practice a century earlier when Gregory IX issued the 'Decretals'. But the system created by John XXII had two cardinal weaknesses. First, it alienated the clergy – or all save that section which profited from it – and condemnation of the church, the great prostitute, the scarlet whore of Babylon, now became widespread. Secondly, it depended implicitly on support from, or a community of interests with, the secular power. So long as king and pope worked together, the opposition of the clergy could be kept under, and both could 'bleed' the church. Co-operation of this sort was already the rule under John XXII; but it had its Achilles' heel, for if the lay power ever turned against the pope, his position would be untenable.

John XXII is deserving of fuller treatment, because he is outstanding among the popes of Avignon, and his pontificate created a system which remained dominant thereafter. The significant thing is that his energy and efficiency solved nothing; and the system he created brought no lasting improvement, even within the limited sphere of administrative procedure to which it was mainly confined. Although *Execrabilis* and other constitutions were reformatory in intention, John's successor, Benedict XII, complained immediately after his accession of the 'innumerable abuses' that had entered the central administration.

Benedict XII (1334–42) was in almost every way the opposite of John XXII. His election marked a deliberate break with the past. To begin with, he was a man of the people, where John had been a born aristocrat. He was also a monk, a Cistercian, who continued to wear his monk's habit after he became pope. As a monk, he was particularly concerned with the reform of the monastic orders – Cistercians, Benedictines, Augustinians, Franciscans and Dominicans – and in fact the great monastic reforms carried out by him constituted a foundation for the future. Few popes have been more bitterly condemned than Benedict XII for hardness, lack of generosity, strictness – a condemnation which is the surest evidence that his measures were effective. His first act as pope was to send home all clergy who were at the curia without specific reason. Later he ordered a thorough review of the bureaucracy of his predecessor. Instead of granting benefices to all and sundry, he preferred to leave livings vacant, rather than fill them with unsatisfactory candidates. He also fixed a limit to the 'procurations', that is, the payments exacted by bishops and other prelates from their subordinates when they visited their dioceses.

68 The east façade of the Palace of the Popes in Avignon; a seventeenth-century drawing

69 Benedict XII,
during whose pontificate
the building of the
Palace of the Popes
was begun

In politics Benedict was definitely pacific; indeed, there is little doubt
that a main consideration in his election was the hope that he would bring
the conflict with Louis of Bavaria to an end. In his first consistory, declaring
his policy, he stated that he never intended to make war, even for the patrimony of the church, except with spiritual arms; adding that the wars which
had been waged in the past by the church had all had an unhappy issue, and
that he placed more confidence in prayers and tears of repentance. But in
fact the negotiations with Louis of Bavaria, which began immediately,
came to nothing, and there is no doubt whatever, in this case, that the cause
was the pressure exerted on the pope by France and Naples, by Philip VI
and Robert of Anjou. That is revealed, quite plainly, by the pope's own
letters and complaints; but it is characteristic that Benedict, in spite of his
own misgivings, saw no alternative save to yield to French threats and
tergiversations. The result was to drive Germany into alliance with England
(26 August 1337), and to produce such a revulsion of feeling in Germany
that the whole country – including the rival dynasties of Luxemburg and
Habsburg – rallied round Louis at the diet of Rhens (1338). As for Benedict
himself, it is clear that he had given up the idea, which had still been a major
factor in John XXII's policy, of returning to Rome. It was he who began
the construction of the great fortress at Avignon, which still overshadows
the town, the Palace of the Popes, which was the symbol of the decision to
remain in Provence.

151

And if Benedict failed in the political field, the other aspect of his policy – internal reform – produced no real change. Even its most lasting achievement, the reform of the monastic orders, relied far too heavily on the regulation of detail, on legal methods, and on a complicated code, which weighed down upon, rather than reviving, the true spirit of religion. His stricter exercise of his power over benefices was sound so far as it went; but – a significant indication of the changing balance of power in the church – he had to make an exception for the cardinals, and so all the light was focussed upon the most glaring abuses. Furthermore, although he was scrupulous in the provisions he made, he extended reservations to cover an even larger number of benefices than any of his predecessors had controlled, and so left added powers for any successor who chose – unlike himself – to use papal control of benefices as a financial and political instrument. Finally, he had the deficiencies of his virtues. Unlike John, he was no businessman and was inefficient in the ordinary routine of administration. John XXII, one chronicler wrote, was extraordinarily rapid in the execution of business; Benedict never got anything done. That was the defect of the system. It required an efficient businessman and organizer to get it done; but an efficient businessman concentrated on administration as though it were an end in itself, and let the greater questions of reform go by default, while a pope who gave attention to the wider issues was all too apt to let the machinery run down and produce administrative chaos. In that sense, as has already been pointed out, a change of personalities or even of policies was not enough to produce remedies, so long as the pope continued to act within the existing system; what was needed was a break with the system itself, but this none, not even the most reformatory, of the popes contemplated.

Benedict XII's successor, Clement VI (1342–52), was again almost completely his opposite. After only six years the cardinals had tired of the rigours of a reformer and unanimously elected a 'grand seigneur', and what is more a Frenchman and a product of the French court. Clement VI had been keeper of the seals in Paris; he had risen in the ecclesiastical hierarchy by service not to the church but to the king of France. Under him, there was no question of an attempt to pursue a policy independent of France. Particularly in relations with Louis of Bavaria, Clement unswervingly followed a French line; and though it is usual to praise his firmness and fixity of purpose, and to assert that his policy was successful in bringing Louis down, in reality it was the political situation within Germany, the complicated ramifications of German territorial policy, rather than the

70 The coronation of Clement VI in the presence of king Philip of France and
Charles of Valois

hostility of the pope, that led to Louis' fall. On the other hand Clement's
subservience to French interests brought the papacy into disrepute; it was
his pontificate which created the common picture of the papacy of Avignon
as an instrument of France.

In the internal affairs of the church in the same way it was Clement VI's
pontificate that branded the papacy of Avignon as profligate, luxurious,
wasteful, and sumptuous. Clement was determined to rule as a great prince.
'My predecessors', he once said, 'did not know how to be popes.' Never
were benefices granted so freely; 'no one', Clement announced, 'should
leave the prince's presence dissatisfied'; 'a pontiff should make his subjects
happy'. His method was lavish grants and lavish expenditure. Money was
spent so freely, or lent to the French king, that the considerable surplus
accumulated by Benedict was soon dissipated; and from Clement's time,   153

in spite of vast revenues and almost exclusive control of the benefices of the whole of western Christendom, the papacy was never free from financial embarrassment, and even reformatory popes – and Clement VI's three successors were all in their way genuine reformers – were driven to financial expedients which further alienated opinion.

The luxury and dissipation of the papal court were now proverbial. Clement's own private morals were notorious, and soon cast a shadow over the papacy as an institution. It is not surprising that it was his pontificate which saw in England the passing of the Statute of Provisors (1351); both his unscrupulous traffic in benefices and his known support of France contrived to bring feeling to a head. But more serious than this ecclesiastico-political opposition – which was soon trimmed to suit the needs of the English king's policy – was the religious opposition, which was fanned by the outbreak of the Black Death. The Black Death seemed to come as God's visitation on a sinful world, but more particularly on a sinful church, and most particularly of all on a sinful papacy. Especially in Germany, where political confusion added to the agitation of spirits, popular religious movements sprang up, of which the best known is the Flagellants – movements seeking to expiate the sins of the day, but which soon turned against the hierarchy, and particularly against ecclesiastical property and the wealth of the church, which seemed – and was – the main cause of evil.

In France the ravages of the Hundred Years War produced the same result. A new wave of genuine religion, coming from below, from the people, sprang to life: a real opportunity for the papacy, if it had known how to use it, but a threat and an omen to the papacy as it was. The religious movement took new forms, and their very newness made them suspect to the hierarchy. Above all, it was a movement of popular sentiment, and therefore hostile to the theological systems built up as the framework of religion by the metaphysicians of the previous century, which were too abstract to warm or comfort the human soul. The essence of the new religion was the concrete historical facts of Christianity – the suffering of Jesus – and the idea of God as a Being, not as a figuration, in philosophical terms, of the Infinite. Devotion, not contemplation, was the keynote: devotion to the Sacred Heart, devotion to the Holy Sacrament, but above all the cult of the Passion. 'The passion of Jesus is no longer an abstract dogma approached by the intelligence; it is a moving image which speaks to the heart.'

The connections of this resurgent devotion with Franciscan piety are evident; but the new religious movement went beyond its model. Its

71, 72 The contrast between the pope and a new upsurge of religion in the fourteenth century. Left, anti-papal caricature of Clement VI. Right, St Catherine of Siena

spirit was expressed best of all by two women – the share of women, whom the church had treated always somewhat contemptuously as the weaker sex, and the source of temptation and evil, is a marked feature of the movement – by St Brigetta of Sweden, daughter of a king, and by St Catherine of Siena, daughter of an artisan. Their letters are full of the bitter joy of mystical union with Christ, and full of devotion to the Virgin; they are also full of criticism, addressing menacing admonishments to Clement, in the name of the Son of God, by whom (they claimed) they had been sent. They are careful to preach submission, even if (says Catherine) the pope is – as she evidently thought he was – a devil incarnate. But then she turns to the attack, begging the pope at long last to do the will of God. If the church has lost its Italian lands, she says, it is because God wants it to return to its primeval state, to the state of the saints who thought not of temporal goods but of the honour of God and the salvation of souls. Answer God's appeal, she admonishes. Take courage; do not leave the servants of God waiting longer. 'Poor miserable creature that I am, I cannot wait longer; life, to me,

73, 74 The decline of the papacy in the fourteenth century was accompanied by a revival of religious fervour among the people. The *Crucifixion* by Giunta Pisano (above) illustrates an increased realism in the artistic treatment of Christ's suffering. The plague, which swept Europe during the century, came to be seen as a punishment for sin. The Flemish miniature at right shows a mass burial of plague-victims is worse than death, when I look and see what outrages are committed against God!'

The plaints of Brigetta of Sweden and of Catherine of Siena may not be objective evidence, but they are testimony to the state of mind left by Clement VI's pontificate; they are not exceptional, only outstanding, witnesses to a widespread disquietude which is reflected in writers and chroniclers everywhere. Clement's three successors, on the other hand, were all men of good character. Innocent VI (1352–62), Urban V (1362–70), and Gregory XI (1370–78) lived soberly, and all three were reformers in spirit; that is to say, they administered the existing system without abuse, sought to reduce the numbers of petitioners for benefices, to keep expenditure within bounds, to issue rules for the religious orders, and to check the greed and materialism of the officials of the curia. But by this time good personal qualities were not enough, and it is useless to dwell in detail on their measures. The real question was the ability of the papacy to keep its head above water in the stormy situation and the general disintegration brought about by the Hundred Years War. The instability resulting from the checkmates of war, which affected all the secular rulers of Europe, now began to affect the pope also; and this in three main directions.

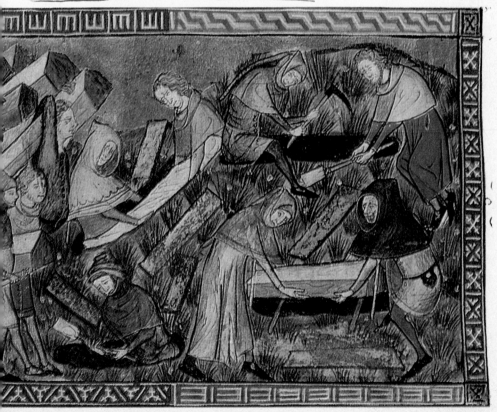

First, the power of the cardinals rose – parallel, for example, with the rise of the power of the aristocracy in England in the latter years of Edward III's reign. Here Clement VI's creations marked a turning-point. After his pontificate, right down to that of Martin V after the Great Schism, the quality of the cardinals as a body – there were naturally always individual exceptions – was not high; but whatever their personal merits or demerits, the decisive fact was that they acted and behaved as princes of the church, similar in many respects to the Italian princes of their period. Secular, aristocratic interests determined their actions. Above all, they were concerned to maintain and build up their own position – to perpetuate the princely régime of Clement VI, from which they had profited.

This attitude was apparent immediately upon Clement VI's death in 1352. In reaction against Clement's worldliness, there was a strong movement to elect the severe, energetic, reformatory general of the Carthusians, Jean Birel, a man of saintly reputation. The cardinals, realizing that reform could only be at their expense, resisted the nomination and instead chose Étienne Aubert, a distinguished teacher of law at the university of Toulouse, but otherwise an insignificant man, satisfactory enough in personal character, but of a hesitating temperament and unlikely to force through drastic measures. On Innocent VI's death in 1362, they actually chose Clement VI's brother; and when he withdrew – realizing the scandal that would arise – they took refuge in the old device of going outside the sacred college, and elected the abbot of St Victor in Marseilles. Urban V was a man of upright character with a high reputation for sanctity – a man who spent himself in prayer, rose early, worked hard and conscientiously – but he was in no sense a radical reformer. And after Urban V, the cardinals unanimously elected the nephew of Clement VI who – a canon of Paris at the age of eleven – had been made cardinal by his uncle at the age of nineteen. Gregory XI was, in fact, in no way like his uncle, Clement. He was modest, pious, studious, but his biographer emphasizes his dependence on the circle round him, and this is the key. He was elected, in other words, as likely to be a willing tool of the cardinals, who were setting out to be the real rulers of the church and to turn the popes into figureheads. The maintenance of that policy under the next pope, Urban VI, was to be the operative cause of the schism. When Urban VI showed signs of carrying reform into the cardinals' college, one of them said to his face: 'Holy Father, you do not treat the cardinals with that honour which you owe to them, as your predecessors did; you are diminishing our honour, and I tell you in all truth that we shall do our best to diminish yours.'

This attitude of the cardinals represented in part their determination to uphold the advantages they had secured under popes like Clement VI; but it also had a theoretical basis which can be traced back into the canon law of the thirteenth century. The pope, after all, was elected by the cardinals; he issued privileges with their advice and assent. In the view of some canonists, his relation to the cardinals was essentially the same as that of any other bishop to his cathedral chapter. It was pointed out that Boniface VIII had annulled grants of bishoprics, abbeys and dignities made by his predecessor, Celestine V, because they were made without the advice of the cardinals, and that Benedict XI had annulled certain statutes of Boniface himself for the same reason. This argument evidently ran contrary to the ordinary interpretation of the pope's plenitude of power; but this theory also was open to more than one interpretation. If some canonists vested the *plenitudo potestatis* in the full possession of the pope – so that the laws (as Boniface VIII was alleged to have said) were in his bosom – others maintained that it was vested in the *ecclesia* as such, i.e., in the whole body of faithful, and that the pope was only the principal minister through whom this power was exercised. The Roman church, it was argued, the *ecclesia Romana*, was not the pope alone; it was constituted of the pope, as head, and of the cardinals, as members, and the obvious corollary was that the one could not act without the other. In other words, the pope could not enact anything without prior consultation with the cardinals.

Conditions at Avignon favoured these views. Even in the twelfth century, as was pointed out earlier, the cardinals had formed a college or corporation, which gave them corporate standing against the pope. As a college, they had their own administration, and in 1289 Nicholas IV had confirmed their right to half of the revenues of the Roman church: i.e., payments made by bishops on appointment, tribute from countries such as Sicily or England, income from the papal states, etc. Although this did not include the new sources of taxation – crusading tithes, annates, and the like – it was a substantial income, which assured them an independent position, and was administered by their own treasury, or *camera*, which was independent of the *camera apostolica*. Their financial position was strengthened even further in 1334, at the beginning of Benedict XII's pontificate, and to maintain their status the number of cardinals was deliberately kept down, so that each cardinal was assured of a substantial income.

During the Avignonese period, when the number of cardinals varied between eighteen and twenty-six, they formed a small and powerful closed corporation, if not a veritable 'senate'. This gave them a position of strength from which they could put pressure on the pope, and this pressure came to a head during the vacancy after the death of Clement VI, when they took the opportunity to draw up a programme, which they swore collectively to observe, so far as was lawful. According to this instrument, known as the electoral capitulation of 1352, the number of cardinals was not to exceed twenty; no new cardinal was to be created until the existing number had fallen to sixteen; none was to be appointed, deposed, or deprived of his rights, without the consent of the college; and no property of the holy see was to be alienated, sold, leased or enfeoffed, save with the assent of two-thirds of the body. In addition, it was laid down that the offices of marshal of the papal court and rector of the lands of the church were never to be conferred on a relative of the pope, and that the approval of the college was necessary for any grant of tithes or subsidies to lay rulers, or for raising taxes on the clergy for the papal treasury; half of any taxes thus raised was to be paid over to the cardinals.

The electoral capitulation of 1352 was not put into effect, for Innocent VI immediately declared it against the law and invalid. But it reveals the oligarchical tendency of the cardinals' policy. Moreover, their strength is shown by the vast sums granted them – as 'gifts' – by the popes on their election: for example, Innocent VI himself, although he annulled the capitulation, paid them 75,000 florins. But more serious was the fact that, in their individual capacities, the cardinals were the clients of lay rulers, paid to put forward their policies at the curia. This was the situation throughout the period beginning with Boniface VIII. It might, of course, express a genuine belief that a particular line of policy was in the best interests of the church; but far too often the cardinals had the position of paid advocates and agents, and pursued a personal policy, which might be contrary to that of the pope, and thus cripple the political action of the holy see. Through the cardinals, kings and rulers – particularly the king of France – sought to use the church as an instrument of policy.

If the growing pretensions of the cardinals and the weakening of the pope in the face of these pretensions was one of the main features after 1352, the second was the growing pressure of the secular rulers. In part, as indicated, this was pressure on the papacy to give them diplomatic support in their policies. But now, owing to the stress under which most rulers found themselves as a result of war and economic regression, there was also pressure to get control over the churches of their lands – over revenues and appointments – in short, to make the church in every kingdom and even in every principality dependent on the ruler, to reduce it to a branch of the state, and so in effect to destroy the 'universality' which had been the mark of the church in the twelfth and thirteenth centuries. No doubt this tendency became more marked after the Great Schism, but its beginnings go back to the Avignonese period. Already in 1364 duke Rudolf IV of Austria had said: 'In my land I will be pope, archbishop, bishop, archdeacon, dean', and this statement sums up a tendency which was widespread throughout Europe in the second half of the fourteenth century.

When similar claims were made by petty princes – by the duke of Bavaria, for example, in 1367 – it is evident that the movement was no longer confined to the great powers – e.g., France – as had been the case at the beginning of the century, but that all secular rulers, however insignificant their territories, felt able to assert their authority against the weakened papacy. First of all, papal overlordship was repudiated: in 1344 by Peter IV of Aragon, in 1366 by England (which had made no payments since 1334). More important, rulers began to lay hands on the church. Already in 1338 the Hungarian bishops complained to Benedict XII that for twenty-three years no bishop had been promoted save at the king's command. In England under Edward II and Edward III the royal *congé d'élire* was equally necessary. The king of Portugal forbade the pope in 1376 to grant bishoprics and appointments of equivalent rank without his consent. In Germany Charles IV, after he succeeded Louis of Bavaria in 1347, got the pope's permission to exercise control over all episcopal nominations in the empire and in Bohemia. In addition, rulers developed what they called the *droit de régale* – the right to administer churches and dioceses and to take the revenues during a vacancy. They reserved for the royal courts all litigation about benefices in which the ruler was concerned. They prohibited the promulgation of papal bulls in their lands without their permission, and forced the clergy – in spite of their privileges – to contribute to taxation.

It was an even more significant development when they began to assert the right to interfere in spiritual matters. Already in 1359, for example, Charles IV ordered the archbishop of Mainz to reform his clergy 'according to the canons'. Even lesser potentates, such as the Black Prince in England – even cities such as Metz – took it upon themselves to reform individual monasteries. Many rulers – for example, the margrave of Brandenburg, Edward III of England, Philip VI of France – ordered prelates to reside in their dioceses; others regulated church-feasts and holidays; many concerned themselves with welfare, care for the poor, and education, which had hitherto been a preserve of the church; and the universities founded at this period – Prague (1348), Vienna (1365), Heidelberg (1386) – were secular foundations. All this shows a rapid advance in the direction of state control; its practical effect was to limit the powers of the papacy, to make its highly developed centralization theoretical rather than practical, and to make it impossible for the pope to act effectively except by agreement with the ruler. There was, at this time, no direct attack on the pope; but in fact he exercised as much power as particular rulers chose to leave him, and this depended, by and large, on what they hoped to get out of him. It would not be long until, during the Great Schism, a spokesman for the university of Paris would say: 'Little does it matter how many popes there are, two or three or ten or a dozen; each kingdom might as well have its own.' No remark could better show the way the papacy had forfeited its historical role; it claimed to be a God-ordained institution, but people thought so little of it that they were quite prepared to do without it.

If the position of the papacy was affected from about 1352 by the rising power of the cardinals, on the one side, and, on the other, by the growth of what is sometimes called 'Erastianism', or state-control, it was affected still more directly by the growing political anarchy and disorder unleashed by the Hundred Years War. After the battle of Poitiers in 1356 the situation in France deteriorated rapidly; and already before the peace of Brétigny, which brought the first phase of the war to a close, many of the companies of freebooters and mercenaries, having no further prospect of profit in France, turned further afield. Some went to Spain, some to Italy, and some entered Provence. This began as early as 1348, and after the conclusion of peace in 1360 it became even worse. In 1364, Urban V had to borrow 30,000 florins to put the defences of Avignon in order. In these circumstances to remain in Avignon became less attractive; and at the same time the English victories, by weakening France, made a return to Italy more possible. But the situation of the papacy in Italy also was parlous. John XXII's policy against the Visconti of Milan, though expensive, had achieved nothing, and the supremacy of the church had ceased to be recognized in the whole of the Romagna. After the death of Robert of Naples in 1343, and the succession of his daughter, the infamous, dissolute and incompetent Joanna, the pope was isolated and without support. The Visconti at Milan were trying to build themselves a Lombard kingdom in the north, and after Robert's death Florence took over leadership in Tuscany and embarked on an aggressive territorial policy.

To go into the ramifications of the Italian situation is unnecessary. Clement VI realized that action was essential if anything at all were to be saved of the papal states; and he sent an army to Italy under his relative,

Durfort. But Durfort was unsuccessful and Clement was forced to come to terms with the Visconti in 1352, and actually to abandon Bologna, the key position, to them. Clement VI's successor, Innocent VI, however, found the right man for the job in the famous Spanish cardinal, Albornóz, a professional soldier and diplomat of first rank who had served against the Moors in Spain before being made cardinal in 1350; and in 1353 Albornóz was sent to Italy as papal commander-in-chief. He was brilliantly successful and in ten years (1353–63) entirely reconquered the papal states.

It was Albornóz's success in occupying Rome that opened the way for the return of the pope to Italy. In 1366, against the pressure of Charles V of France and of the cardinals, Urban V decided to return, and actually got as far as Viterbo, when the death of Albornóz (22 August 1367) threw the whole situation into the melting-pot again, and in 1370 the pope was forced to withdraw to Avignon. Although this was a serious setback, the die was cast. Urban's successor, Gregory XI, although dominated by the cardinals, was well aware that a return to Italy was imperative if the papal states were to be saved. Another general, Robert of Geneva (the future pope Clement VII), was sent to prepare the way. He came to terms with the English mercenary Hawgood and the Breton free companies, neutralized the Visconti by diplomacy, and isolated Florence. France again made efforts in 1375 to hold the pope back, and for the moment with success; Gregory had announced his impending departure in the autumn of 1374, but gave way to French pressure. But this intervention provoked an Italian nationalist revolt, stimulated by the growing humanism. There were anti-papal risings throughout the states of the church, in Tuscany, Romagna, Campania, the March of Ancona, and a general swing of the pendulum away from the papacy to the side of Florence. Whatever else, the Italians were determined no longer to remain under the rule of French rectors, administering the Italian territories for an absent pontiff.

75, 76 Urban V decided in 1366 to return to Rome (below), but got only as far as Viterbo. Left, the Papal Loggia of the Bishop's Palace

Their pressure was decisive, and at the end of 1375 Gregory determined to leave. There was still opposition from France, still intrigues among the cardinals, and above all difficulty in collecting the necessary finance. Finally, in August 1376, the Romans sent an embassy to Gregory, saying that if he did not come, they would proceed to the election of another pope. This threat decided the issue. In September 1376 the pope went on board ship, and in January 1377 he arrived in Rome. The period of the Avignonese papacy had ended. But, as a French historian has said, 'this success, unlike the victory of Gregory VII, was not due to the support of the Christian conscience everywhere; it was a result of the opposition of Italian nationalism to France and to French policy'. Furthermore, the return of the papacy to Rome altered nothing. The forces which had dominated since 1352 went on dominating; the pope's position was not strengthened; and the pope's return to Rome only added another to the existing causes of tension and weakness – the hostility between the French and the Italians, and between the pro-French and the anti-French forces in Europe. By returning to Rome, the papacy did not recover its independence; having long been an instrument, it simply became a plaything in European politics. The immediate result was not an improvement in the pope's position, but schism; and it was not until the end of the schism and the election of pope Martin V in 1417 – perhaps not until thirty years later, in 1447 – that a new period in the history of the papacy began. In the meantime, the situation deteriorated in every way; indeed, it may be said that the schism between 1378 and 1417 marked the end of the medieval papacy and the beginning of the 'Renaissance papacy', which lasted until the council of Trent, meeting between 1545 and 1563, inaugurated the period of the regenerated papacy of the Counter-Reformation.

THE GREAT SCHISM

It was evident already before the event that the death of Gregory XI was likely to produce a difficult situation. Gregory himself, fully aware of the perils facing the church, took steps to prepare the way by authorizing the majority of cardinals actually present at his court at the time of his death – that is, actually in Italy – to proceed immediately to the choice of a successor, and in this way to avoid the dangers of a long vacancy while those members of the college absent in France and elsewhere gathered together. There was no doubt that the French king would renew pressure; and it was also certain that the Romans, who were aroused, would demand the election of a Roman. When Gregory XI died on 27 March 1378, the assembled cardinals compromised by going outside the college once again, and – though not electing a Roman – they chose an Italian, the archbishop of Bari, who became pope Urban VI on 8 April. All witnesses agreed in praising his high moral qualities, his fervour for reform, and his experience of practical affairs. Later his uncompromising demands produced a reaction against him; but it was certainly a worthy choice in a by no means easy situation.

Two factors already familiar, lay pressure and the attitude of the cardinals, conspired to ruin this auspicious beginning in only a few months; or three factors, if we include the pope's own personality. Urban VI, who had never been a cardinal, was much more alive than the cardinals were to the general criticism of the papacy, and was determined to meet the criticism from the very beginning, and to set an example, by reforming the curia, beginning with the cardinals' college itself. He was determined also to use the full plenitude of papal power to achieve this end; it was, he thought, the only way to break down the opposition of vested interests. The result was that he came into head-on collision with the cardinals, whose oligarchic pretensions he threatened. But conflict between pope and cardinals was nothing new – it had happened in the case of Boniface VIII and the Colonna, for example – and something more was needed to lead to schism. The additional factor was the question of nationalism. What made it possible for the cardinals to resist Urban successfully, was the support of France, reacting against an Italian papacy and the weakening of France's diplomatic position which an Italian papacy portended.

The spokesman for France was the cardinal-bishop of Amiens, a member of Charles V's council, who arrived in Rome too late for the election, but proceeded to whip up the discontent of the cardinals into open revolt. Urban VI was elected on 8 April 1378; already on 2 August, thirteen discontented cardinals called upon him to abdicate. Six weeks later, on 20 September, they elected a new pope, a cousin of the king of France, and the man who had succeeded Albornóz as military commander in Italy: Robert of Geneva, who took the title of Clement VII. So began the schism.

It would be hard – though the attempt has been made – to justify the attitude of the thirteen rebellious cardinals. Urban had been duly elected, without protest of any sort. Clement VII was simply a nominee of France and of a French faction among the cardinals. He had the support only of France and of those countries which gravitated in a French orbit – Scotland, Naples, Castile, Aragon – while the anti-French powers (England, Scandinavia, Germany, Italy apart from Naples, and the Catholic states of eastern

Europe) supported Urban. Even in France it needed all the pressure Charles V could exert to persuade the university of Paris to acknowledge the royal candidate. The haughtiness of Urban VI – which his troubles accentuated – was a factor favouring Clement; but had it not been in harmony with French political interests and ambitions, the rival party could not have lasted many weeks.

For France what was involved was its Italian policy, inaugurated a century earlier by Charles of Anjou and continued a century later by Charles VIII. Clement VII was used as a tool to further this policy. Charles V's brother, Louis of Anjou, was sent to Italy to win the 'kingdom of Adria' which Clement had promised him, and to secure the succession to Naples. Urban VI and his successor Boniface IX were the figureheads of Italian resistance to these French designs. In this way the papacy became the puppet of European politics; it was made to serve purposes and interests foreign to its own intrinsic functions. That this was possible was the result of its gradual depression during the Avignonese period.

The significant thing was the reaction this situation provoked. This reaction took two forms. First, it gave added impetus to those – and they were a growing number – who rejected the hierarchy as corrupt, and sought to free religious life from the hierarchical apparatus that was disfiguring it. This was a movement away from the sacraments and back to the Bible, which alone was infallible. Back to the Bible meant away from the 'doctors', the schoolmen, who claimed to interpret it; away from ecclesiastical tradition and the visible church, the repository (as it claimed to be) of that tradition, which set out to be the only legitimate intermediary between the Bible and the individual. Much of this protest was old; we have seen it gathering at the turn of the thirteenth and fourteenth centuries.

77 Sarcophagus of Urban VI (1378–89), during whose pontificate the great schism between Rome and Avignon began

78 Pope Boniface IX (1389–1404), Urban VI's successor in the 'Roman obedience' and, like him, a Neapolitan by birth; as popular as Urban was unpopular, but a notorious simoniac whose exactions brought the papacy into disrepute

But the circumstances of the times gave it a new cogency. For now it was plain that the papacy could err; was it not, after all, the papal curia that was guilty of the ruin which the schism portended?

Two figures, above all others, expressed this aspect of the religious ferment: John Wycliffe and John Hus. Of the two, Wycliffe was the original thinker, but Hus was the effective force, if only because conditions in Bohemia provided material for a revolutionary outburst. Hence the Hussite movement quickly emerged as the great overriding issue of the day. Behind all the ecclesiastico-political events of the time, behind the great councils, and driving them ever on, was the shadow of the Hussite movement, spreading far and wide outside the boundaries of Bohemia – a visible sign of what awaited a church that was unable to put its house in order. It is impossible to understand the conciliar movement if one's view is confined only to what happened at Pisa and Constance, at Basel and Florence; it is necessary all along to remember Hussitism in the background – a sort of thunder, never far away, which accompanies the reformers on their task.

79, 80 Precept and practice: two miniatures from a Hussite manuscript, contrasting Christ as the servant of his disciples and the pope with minions at his feet

The first result of the schism, therefore, was the stimulus it gave to reformers – for Wycliffe and Hus were, of course, reformers in spirit rather than revolutionaries – who rejected the church as it was, to get back to a purer form of Christianity without the accretions which had encumbered it through the passage of time. The second reaction – stimulated by the Hussite movement – was that of men who quickly came to see that something must be done, if rejection of the church were not to become universal. What is remarkable is how quick and how widespread this reaction was, and how it was able to overrule political interests. At first, we have seen, the French king had forced the university of Paris into the camp of Clement VII; but he was unable to keep it there. At the end of his life Charles V of France acknowledged his guilt, and accepted the demand of the university for a general council to find a way out. Similarly the cardinals. It took them a long time to act, and meanwhile things went from bad to worse; but in the end, in 1408, cardinals from both obediences got together, and summoned the first of the general councils, the council of Pisa.

The conciliar movement was thus the result of a general stirring of the Christian conscience. Conciliar ideas had a long history; there had always been a tendency – as far back as the time of the conflict between Frederick II and Innocent IV – to appeal from the pope to a future general council. But conciliar ideas were not prominent at the beginning of the schism. There had been no general council since 1311, and since then the course of development had moved in a contrary direction, towards a greater and greater concentration of power in the pope and the curia. It was only gradually after 1378 that conciliar theory won adherents, as it became obvious that a general council was the only course which offered any hope of a solution. Among those who propounded conciliar theories were radical critics of the papacy. But the support the idea of summoning a general council won from kings, prelates and cardinals shows that it was not intended to be a radical or revolutionary step, but simply a practical measure for getting out of a practical impasse – a measure regretfully and hesitantly adopted, but adopted nevertheless because there seemed to be – and probably was – no feasible alternative.

81, 82 Hussite propaganda. Left, monks and nuns disporting together in a monastery garden. Right, an exhortation to temperance in pleasure and religion

This fact should always be borne in mind in considering the history of the great councils. It explains – together, of course, with political under-currents which were never far below the surface – what seem to us often to be their half-measures and compromises, and their failure to adopt radical remedies to shear the papacy of its power. The reason was that only a minority saw the pope and the council (as many modern historians have seen them) as antagonists fighting to the death for contrary principles. Few of those most closely involved regarded support for the council as equiva-lent to hostility to the papacy, though it might imply hostility to one or all of the claimants to the papal throne. They thought of the council rather as a means to help the papacy to set its house in order. It was characteristic that the council of Constance sought to prove its orthodoxy by condemning and burning John Hus; it deliberately dissociated itself from the radical attack on the existing order in the church which the Lollard and Hussite movements embodied.

It may be that this moderation was a weakness; that the councils would have prospered better and achieved more if they had taken up the popular demand for an evangelical church modelled on the structure of primitive Christianity. But such criticism is really beside the point. The princes and prelates, who were the dominating element, were also people in authority, and consciously or subconsciously they were aware that an attack on the pope's authority might unleash an attack on authority as such, which would be to their detriment. This, after all, was what happened in Bohemia. But it was not merely a question of self-interest. More important in the long run was the fact that the councils did not feel it was their task to kick the pope when he was down; rather their job was to help him to get up again, and then to get things working 'normally'. In fact, the idea of a return to 'normalcy' was an illusion, then as always; the result of the councils was not a return to the old order, but the advance of the papacy to a new position. But that does not alter the fact that the underlying motive was to restore what the schism had dislocated.

All in all, therefore, the conciliar movement was far more conservative than we are apt to concede. Naturally this conservatism left room for differences. First of all, even very conservative men might have more than one view of what was 'normal'. There was also the question how far an un-controlled exercise of papal powers – even if those powers were legitimate in themselves – had contributed to the breakdown from which the papacy itself was the worst sufferer, and therefore whether in the interests of the papacy itself a definition or redefinition of papal powers was desirable or necessary. And finally there was the question how far it was possible to get back to 'normal' without reform; whether, in short, a mere healing of the schism could produce a lasting settlement, seeing that the schism – as men came more and more to believe – was only the result, and not the cause, of the evils afflicting the church. It was Nicholas de Clemanges, one of the most level-headed thinkers of the time, and a firm opponent of the council of Constance – a man, in short, who had no inclination to go out of his way to criticize the papacy – who said, quite openly: 'If the Roman church had not arrogated to itself the disposition over benefices of all ranks throughout the universal church, and had not despoiled all other churches, throttling their rights with its, this schism would never have occurred or, if it had occurred, would never have lasted so long.'

Clemanges' observations are significant. They show how the question of healing the schism led on, almost of necessity, to the question of reform. And that, in fact, was the direction in which events moved. But the question of healing the schism was always predominant over the question of reform. Against those who believed that reform was the only remedy for schism, there were always those who thought that the schism was the cause of trouble; and this cleavage was decisive in the outcome. To get a single, universally recognized pope in the saddle again, to give him the means to put things right, and above all to combat the growing heresy – which really did imply a demand for radical change in the ecclesiastical constitution – that, for the majority, was enough. Reform was really a means to an end, not an end in itself.

In any case, the cleavage within the councils – particularly in the later phase, at Basel – and the hesitation to take radical measures, which might have encouraged the Hussites, helped the papacy in the end to defeat the reforming wing. Whether it was wise for the papacy to take that line, whether in its own interests it should have rejected moderate reform, is a more difficult question. It is not easy to think that the papacy had anything to lose by co-operating with the councils, whose proposals were extra-ordinarily moderate. No attack was made on the secular basis of papal power – that was the position of the heretics whom the councils condemned – nor was there any demand for evangelical poverty. All that was asked was for the papacy to put its house in order. Indeed, it is a valid criticism of the councils that they paid so little heed to the fundamental issues ventilated in earlier generations – to the arguments of the Spiritual Franciscans, for example – and concentrated instead on purely practical questions of limited scope: how to enable the papacy to live on the revenues from its landed possessions (the rightfulness of which was not contested), or how to ensure an adequate income for the pope without using benefices simply as a means of filling an empty treasury, and yet to leave the pope with his powers of conferment unchecked in principle.

These and similar proposals may scarcely have brought about a total reform of the church; but they were not fundamentally irreconcilable with papal claims. They showed, in Haller's words, that the councils had no intention of emptying out the baby with the bath; and it is a serious criticism of the popes that none made any attempt to see whether the conciliar programme would work. In this way they missed the last chance for reform, while there was still time – for voluntary reform. Later, at the council of Trent, they had to make concessions as radical as anything that would have been required at the time of Constance or Basel; but by the time of Trent they were under the pressure of Protestantism, and it was this pressure – and this pressure alone – which forced them to revise their attitudes and abandon practices which, if they had voluntarily surrendered them earlier, might have saved the situation.

That, really, was the tragedy of the medieval papacy. The conciliar movement gave it its last opportunity. The trouble with the popes was that they were too clever to take it, but not clever enough to see the consequences of not taking it. Their efforts were concentrated on out-manœuvring the council, when they should have been profiting from the fervour for the welfare of the church – which, behind all the intrigues and political jockeying for position, was a real force throughout the conciliar epoch – to restore their position. The result was a tactical victory, which only increased the distance between the papacy and the body of the faithful. There was not much anti-papal feeling of a positive sort in the second half of the fifteenth century; but there was real indifference. Contrary to what is often thought, the turn of the fifteenth and sixteenth centuries was a time of exceptional religious fervour and activity, of deep orthodox piety, and in many parts of Europe of genuine reforming zeal; but it was a religious life in which the papacy – more and more severed from the general life of the church since 1447 – had no part to play. In the last analysis, it was this failure, the failure to give a lead and to take command of the swelling religious currents – as Innocent III, for example, had taken command of the Franciscan movement at a similar turning-point in the history of the church – that left the way open for Luther, who succeeded precisely because he gave the deep piety of the age an objective outside itself, which was lacking.

It remains to trace, very briefly, the course of events which led to this result.

At first there was no question of reform, no question of summoning a council, and very little thought of healing the schism. The two popes, with secular backing, were prepared to fight it out; and their supporters, particularly Charles V of France, were prepared to give them the means. The question of a general council, to settle the issue, was first raised, in 1380–81, by two German masters at the university of Paris, Conrad of Gelnhausen and Henry of Langenstein. They argued that the infallibility of the church was incarnated not in the pope, but in the community of the faithful, and that the general council, as the representative of the community of the faithful, was superior to the pope. Whatever the relations between the universal church and the Roman church in normal times, in a crisis the former was superior to the latter. Furthermore, in such circumstances, it was the duty of the princes – for who else was there? – to summon a council for the common good, and bring the schism to an end.

But the arguments of Conrad of Gelnhausen and Henry of Langenstein were premature. The king of France was still backing Clement VII up to the hilt, and was prepared to force the university of Paris to conform; the two masters were forced to depart, the one to Heidelberg, the other to Vienna. It needed the passage of time and a rapid deterioration in the situation before Conrad's and Henry's views began to gather support. Only the pressure of circumstances forced people in the direction of a council. Above all, the cardinals on both sides were hostile to it. If, as we have seen, their oligarchic pretensions had been a main cause of the schism, it was not likely

83 Effigy of Charles V of France (1364–80), one of the main fomenters of the schism

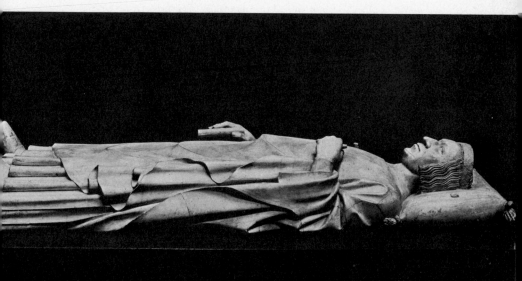

that they would willingly abdicate power into the hands of a council; if anyone were to have power to decide, in their view it should be they. But, outside the college of cardinals – or rather the two colleges – there was little support for an oligarchic form of church government, since it was recognized that the cardinals themselves were in large measure at fault, and no one wanted to change papal rule for rule by a cardinals' senate. Nevertheless, the idea of a council was not popular, particularly among kings, who preferred, if it were possible, to end the schism by what they called the *via cessionis*, i.e., by forcing one claimant or the other, under pressure, to abdicate. It was only when this proved impossible, and simultaneously everything got worse, that a council became practical politics.

This occurred only in the second phase, after the two protagonists had passed away. Urban VI died in 1389, but was immediately succeeded by another Neapolitan, Boniface IX, who was as popular as Urban was unpopular, and who quickly improved the position of the Roman obedience. But by now the exactions of both parties were beginning to work on opinion. Boniface IX, on the Roman side, was the most notorious simoniac in the whole history of the papacy, far outdoing any of the popes of Avignon; anything and everything had its price. But Clement VII was not much better, and in fact the situation – the continuous war both popes were involved in for control of Italy, and the reduplication of the whole unwieldy bureaucracy – made financial extortion on an unparalleled scale almost inevitable.

The result was a general reaction, a feeling on all sides that the popes were ruining the church – which was literally true – and a change of spirit which becomes evident about 1390. It was helped by changes in the French government after the death of Charles V, the real promoter of the schism, in 1380. He was succeeded by a weak youth, Charles VI, under whom government was in fact in the hands of his uncles. In these circumstances the attitude of the French court began to fluctuate. Louis, duke of Orleans, who hoped to receive an Italian kingdom from Clement VII, remained his determined supporter; but from about 1384 his influence was countered by that of Philip of Burgundy, who had established his rule in Flanders in 1384, and whose interest it was not to oppose the Roman pope whom his Flemish subjects recognized. Thus, at the crucial moment, the Burgundian question became involved with the papal question. The university of Paris, led by the famous Jean Gerson, and emboldened by Philip of Burgundy, took up an anti-Clementine policy in 1391. Though repelled twice and ordered to keep silence, in 1394 the masters of the university were asked to suggest a remedy, and proposed three possible methods: the simultaneous cession of both popes, arbitration between them, or, finally, a general council. They were resentful of the spoliation of the French church and also genuinely convinced that, in supporting Clement, France was wrong. But their move had no immediate effect; they were again ordered not to interfere. When, however, Clement died a few months later (10 September 1394), the French court decided to withdraw support and ordered the cardinals of Avignon not to elect a successor, but instead to support Boniface IX and thus to end the schism.

From that point events moved quickly. The cardinals at Avignon refused to accept French orders, and immediately elected an Aragonese, Peter de Luna, as Benedict XIII. Although Charles VI of France never ceased to vacillate, the effect in France was considerable, for the election was a rebuff to French policy. Moreover, England and France were at peace at the time, and so France had less need or use for a pope of its own. A further council at Paris in 1395 called on the pope to heal the schism by 'cession', but Benedict refused. This demand was seconded by a joint Anglo-French-Castilian delegation in 1397, but this also was ignored; and then, to put pressure on the pope, a third council, again at Paris, suggested what is known as the 'subtraction of obedience', i.e., withdrawal of obedience, and therewith of any papal interference in the church of France; in other words, it deprived Benedict of the means to govern.

The subtraction of obedience in 1398 was an important event in more directions than one. First, it marked a definite swing in French policy: France still, of course, wanted a French pope; but it did not want, because it could really not profit from, a pope who was recognized only in France and in states which were French clients. Little was to be gained by that. Therefore French policy veered away from schism to unity, and to the search for a universally recognized pope who could support French interests universally. Secondly, the 'subtraction' had significant effects on the French clergy. Whatever they may have expected – the abolition, perhaps, of the pope's rights, of taxes and provisions and appeals, and the restoration of the old powers of the bishops – what happened in fact was that the French crown stepped in, and took over for its own use all the pope's prerogatives. Benefices simply went to the king's nominees or those of the princes, instead of to the pope's; the clergy paid as much, or more, to the king than they had paid to the papal *camera*.

The reaction was twofold. Those who suffered – and they were many – and those whose consciences were disturbed by this advance of the lay power – and they also were many – came more than ever to see that the restoration of unity was an urgent necessity. Those, on the other hand, who benefited – royal clerks and time-servers at the royal court, also in large degree the university of Paris, which was closely associated with the administration, but not the provincial universities – accustomed themselves to royal control. They saw its advantages for them, and got used to the idea of a national church, catholic but administered on a national basis. The Gallican church, they discovered, was capable of governing itself without the pope; and this was to be of the greatest importance for the future. The measures to administer the church of France introduced in consequence of the subtraction of obedience in 1398 became the practical basis of 'Gallicanism' which lasted through the age of Louis XIV down to the French Revolution.

Owing to fluctuations at the French court the 'subtraction' of obedience was discontinued in 1403; but from 1405 the university of Paris again began to agitate against Benedict. The theologian Jean Petit demanded a total withdrawal of obedience. But a more moderate solution was put forward by Peter d'Ailly – namely, to recognize the pope's spiritual authority, but to deny his temporal authority. D'Ailly's view prevailed, and was adopted on 4 January 1407. The king's officers immediately drew up ordinances, ready on 18 February, for the administration of the Gallican church; and after Benedict had provoked the king by a threat of excommunication, they were published on 14 May 1408. These ordinances set out the 'liberties of the Gallican church', and were of lasting significance. Unlike the ordinances of 1398, which were only a means to an end, the 'liberties of the Gallican church' became an integral part of French constitutional law. No future pope, however legitimate, could ignore them. In addition, they provided an example for other kings and princes: what France had done, they could do also.

These were long-term results. The immediate result was that France declared itself neutral between the two popes, and this declaration without doubt facilitated further developments. Meanwhile, in Rome, Boniface IX had died in 1404, his successor Innocent VI in 1406, and the Roman cardinals had elected an aged Venetian, Gregory XII, on the understanding – to which, however, he only gave a very ambiguous assent – that he would abdicate if the cardinals of both obediences met together to elect a single pope. The cardinals still hoped to settle the schism themselves, and so to retain a decisive voice. But the stubbornness of the two popes prevented such a solution; and the pressure of events, particularly the declaration of

Gallican liberties and the threat it carried with it of a permanent loss of papal resources, which would have hit the cardinals almost as badly as the pope himself, forced their hand.

If neither pope would resign, how could they be got rid of? The difficulty about a council was that it should be summoned by the pope, but if there were no universally recognized pope, this was impossible. Spokesmen in the university had put forward the idea that, in the crisis, it was for rulers to step in and take the initiative; but this was obviously repulsive to ecclesiastical minds, and particularly to the cardinals. In the end, to avoid worse, the cardinals of the two obediences – both out of patience with their uncompromising pontiffs – got together and of their own authority summoned a council at Pisa (1409). From a strictly legal point of view, their authority to do so was non-existent – if neither of the rival popes was legitimate, how could the cardinals they had created be so either, and whence did they derive their authority? – but the situation was their justification. Nevertheless, the doubtfulness of their title was an inherent weakness. The two popes were declared schismatics and heretics, and deposed; a new pope, Alexander V, was set up, but no one was particularly keen to accept his authority, which derived from a doubtfully legitimate assembly. Hence the net result of the council was to add a third to the contending claimants, and when Alexander V died in 1410 matters were not improved, for the cardinals immediately elected a successor, the energetic but irreligious soldier, Baldassare Cossa, as pope John XXIII.

84 Pope John XXIII, before his elevation the *condottiere* Baldassare Cossa, who was deposed at the council of Constance in 1415 and died after imprisonment in 1419

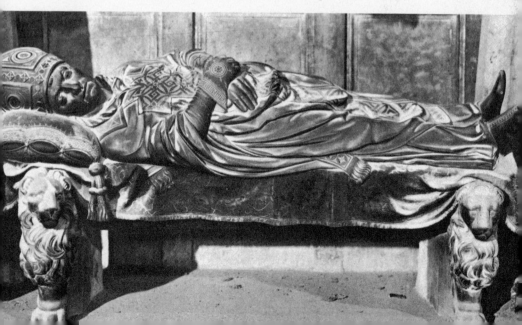

What brought about a change was the situation in a country which hitherto had played little part in the politics of the schism: Germany. When the schism broke out, Germany was being governed – or rather misgoverned – by the shiftless son of Charles IV, Wenzel or Wenceslaus. The result was that Germany was a nullity down to 1400, when the electors deposed Wenzel; but by electing Rupert of the Palatinate, a petty western prince, without real power, they made things no better. The turning-point came in 1410 with Rupert's death and the election of Wenzel's more able brother, Sigismund. For Sigismund, whose power depended on his hereditary estates in Bohemia, the Hussite wars and the Bohemian revolt were a deadly challenge, threatening to undermine his whole position; and Sigismund had a vital interest in healing the schism in order to divert the efforts of a united Christendom against the Hussites. He therefore quickly took up the demand, now widespread, for a general council, and with his backing the idea, which hitherto had failed because of the hesitation of kings and cardinals, became practical politics. Profiting from a turn of fortunes in Italy, which forced John XXIII to seek his support, he extracted from the pope a promise to summon a council at Constance, and held him to his word. At the end of 1414, much to the pope's distaste, the council he had summoned met.

85, 86 Jan Hus, condemned as a heretic by the council of Constance, was burnt and his ashes scattered in 1415 (above left). Right, Jan Žižka at the head of the Hussite army which continued the religious and national struggle with surprising success

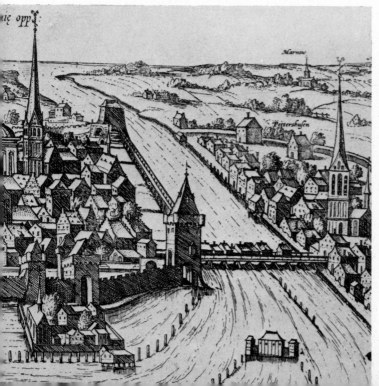

87 Constance, scene of the council which lasted from 1414 to 1418, as it appeared at the end of the sixteenth century

The council of Constance deliberated in a number of sessions from 1414 to 1418; but it disappointed the high hopes it had raised. On two things only was there agreement: the deposition of the contending popes (Gregory XII, in fact, resigned and was not deposed) and the condemnation of Hus, who had attended under safe-conduct. The burning of Hus – a public demonstration that the council had no leaning to heretical views – was inauspicious enough. And nothing else went well. The German ruler alone had any practical interest in reform. France, safe behind the barrier of the 'Gallican liberties', and England behind that of the 'anti-papal legislation' of the fourteenth century, were satisfied with the *status quo*; they had secured all they wanted from the pope, and had no wish to depreciate his standing further. The Italians, who regarded the papacy after its return from Avignon as their affair, did not desire a diminution of its rights, which might be to Italian disadvantage; and the cardinals also were bound to the existing system by the advantages it gave them.

Only the outbreak of war between England and France and the French defeat at Agincourt (1415) allowed Sigismund to make any progress at all. Fearing the numerical superiority of the French and Italians, Sigismund had introduced a system of voting by nations – English, German, French, Italian and (later) Spanish – but even this availed him nothing because the English, under the pious and orthodox Henry V, in the end deserted him on the crucial issue. This was whether or not to proceed with the election of a new pope before carrying through reform. By deciding, against Sigismund's advice, to proceed to the election first, the other nations really decided the fate of the council. The papalist party, having got rid of its disreputable popes, was taking heart again; and in November 1417 an Italian of the famous house of Colonna was elected pope as Martin V.

As a compromise a few decrees to which there was general assent were passed in advance of the election; the most important laid down that in future general councils should meet at stated intervals, the first after five, the second after seven, and others after ten years. The council also drew up a list of headings for reform after a pope was elected, and stipulated that the new pope, before the council dissolved, should agree in principle on the reforms needed. It was all tepid, and placed no real control – as he well knew – over Martin V, who contented himself with reassuring declarations of a general nature. Instead of reformatory decrees, Martin negotiated, and the council approved, concordats with the individual nations – the English concordat permanent, the others for five years – which (on paper at least) gave back the pope some of his powers, but confirmed the lay rulers in theirs. More important, they had the effect of weaning the kings from reform, for why press for radical measures, if they could get all they wanted by diplomacy?

So far as reform was concerned, the council of Constance failed, partly because of dissension, partly because the members, frightened of being denounced as revolutionaries, drew back from radical measures, but most of all owing to the play of secular politics. Voting by nations placed power in the hands of governments, and split the reformatory circles which otherwise might have joined together to push through some fundamental changes; it left the last word with the princes, whose chief aim in matters ecclesiastical was mastery over their own national churches. Certainly, they were weary of the confusion caused by the schism, and so they ended it; they were also averse to the competition of papal taxation, and so they limited it; but their attitude to general reform – the effect of which would have been to make the church less subservient to the crown – was dubious and tepid, and so it was left undone.

The next council, at Pavia (1423), achieved nothing at all; it was held only for form, to prove that Martin V was abiding by the ruling of Constance. The council of Basel proved different. No doubt, here again Martin V hoped to do nothing; but the astounding military successes of the Hussites, culminating in their victory over the Germans at Taus in 1431, convinced Cardinal Cesarini, whom Martin had appointed to take charge of the preparations, that only real reform could check the advance of heresy, and when the council met a few weeks later at the end of 1431, Cesarini threw himself into the work with energy and good will. Only a thorough and rapid reform of the clergy, he warned the pope, would prevent the laity from following the Hussites' example. The cardinal's conversion – he had been singularly lukewarm at first – is a remarkable sign of the new sense of urgency, and by taking the lead – often against the recalcitrant pope – Cesarini became the outstanding figure. He worked in close harmony with the emperor Sigismund, who also had everything to gain by a settlement of the Bohemian question, and in this way he was able to force the pope's hand.

A week or two after authorizing Cesarini to act, Martin V died and was succeeded by Eugenius IV (1431–47), a respectable man but a mediocrity, obstinate and determined, no matter how, to out-manœuvre the council. Above all else, he was frightened of any compromise with the Bohemian heretics, although, as Cesarini and Sigismund knew, it was impossible to defeat them by arms and a compromise was unavoidable. When the

88 Martin V (1417–31), whose pontificate marked the end of the schism and the beginning of the restoration of the ecclesiastical and temporal power of the papacy

council invited the Hussite leaders to attend, Eugenius therefore declared it dissolved (December 1431). This, he was well aware, was a declaration of war; and the council – now supported by all the leading powers, including England and France – took up the challenge, eventually forcing the pope to withdraw and finally, in December 1433, to promise co-operation.

Without any doubt, it was Eugenius who drove the council, step by step, to a radical position. If, in December 1433, he gave way, it was because the council had been successful in its negotiations with the Hussites, and he realized what a blow it would be for the papacy if this success appeared to have been achieved in spite of its opposition. The so-called 'Compacts of Prague', agreed in November 1433, were in reality the result of a split within the Hussite movement between the more conservative Czech nobility and the body of the people; and even after the defeat of the latter in the following year the religious and social ferment in Bohemia continued. Nevertheless, from the point of view of the council, the Compacts of Prague were a turning-point, for Sigismund, hitherto its strongest supporter, had now got what he wanted and concentrated his efforts on an attempt to restore his position in Bohemia, leaving the council pretty well to its own devices. His death in 1437 was the end of a chapter. His heir, Albert of Austria, died suddenly in 1439, and the electors chose another member of the Austrian house, Frederick III, to succeed. But the Austrian inheritance, divided and subdivided among different branches, was at this stage very insecure, and the result was that the empire, which had shown signs of revival under Sigismund, fell back into anarchy. Not only did Frederick not support the council, but, owing to his financial weakness, he was ready to reach an understanding with the pope. And the same applied to the other main powers. England, which had got all it wanted by the concordat of 1418 with Martin V, soon veered over to the side of Eugenius. In France, which was now emerging triumphantly from the Hundred Years War and in a position to assert itself once again, the decrees of the council with regard to papal taxation and the disposal of benefices were taken over in the famous Pragmatic Sanction of Bourges (1438) and made a law of the French state; from that time forward France also, which in this way reaped for itself the harvest sown by the councils, had little further interest.

Two further developments contributed to the outcome. First, the council, seeing itself abandoned by the secular powers, felt a new sense of urgency and pressed on ever more radically with reform; but the result was to alienate opinion and to strengthen the conservative elements which wanted to see papal power regulated, but not destroyed. By setting up rival courts, claiming papal taxes, and interfering in the central administration of the church, the council certainly went beyond what most people were ready to accept: this was not reform, but simply the transfer of the existing apparatus to a new head – the council. Thus the papal cause began to revive. Secondly, just as the Hussite question had led to a defeat for the pope, a second question of a similar character contributed to his success. This was the question of the Greek church which, hard pressed by the Turks, looked

89 Sigismund receives the imperial crown from Eugenius IV (1433)

90 Seal of the council of Basel (1431–49)

91 Coronation by pope Nicholas V of the emperor Frederick III in 1452; this was the last crowning of an emperor of the Holy Roman Empire in Rome ▶

to the west for help. Eugenius saw the opportunity this gave him and grasped it. The Greeks badly wanted papal support, had no use for the council, and wanted to negotiate in Italy. But the council – which also wanted the prestige of settling this issue – dared not go to Italy, where it would find itself under the pope's guns. The issue split the council. Cesarini, who had been its mainstay, was prepared to go to Italy; with a minority he moved to Ferrara, and thence to Florence, where in 1439 the reunion of the Greek and Latin churches was effected.

Meanwhile, the majority in Basel, composed largely of representatives of the lower clergy and the universities, adopted an increasingly extreme and anti-papal attitude, actually deposing Eugenius and electing in his place the former duke of Savoy as Felix V (1439). But after 1439 the council, though it continued in existence for another decade, was for all practical purposes a dead letter. Most of the princes had already gone over to the pope's side. Finally, in 1446, Frederick III, in serious financial straits, also sold his adhesion to Eugenius in exchange for the right to nominate to certain bishoprics, and for a cash payment. In the end the death of Eugenius IV (1447) and the election of a new pope, Nicholas V, who was not so personally involved and obnoxious as Eugenius had been, paved the way for pacification. In February 1448 the new pope and Frederick III concluded the concordat of Vienna, which gave the German ruler much the same privileges as the western powers had already obtained, and in 1452 Nicholas crowned Frederick emperor in Rome. Thus their reconciliation was sealed. But by then the council of Basel, more and more isolated and abandoned to its own devices, had declared itself dissolved. When in 1460 Pius II branded any appeal to a general council as heresy and treason, another chapter was closed. The attempt to reform the medieval papacy had failed.

The period of the councils brought great and decisive changes in the life and constitution of the church, but not in the direction expected nor of the character most reformers had desired. The attempt at reform and a re-definition of the pope's place in the church had come to nothing; but the result was not, and could not be, a return to the past. Instead the papacy embarked on a new course, symbolized by the move from the Lateran palace to the Vatican. The reconstruction of the Vatican, begun by Nicholas V in 1447, marked a change not merely of the seat but also of the principles of papal government, and an even more obvious expression of the new spirit was the building of the new St Peter's, the foundation-stone of which was laid in 1506. With the displacement of the basilica of St John Lateran by St Peter's and the Vatican a new period of papal history began.

This new period reflected the changes which had taken place since 1378. Though other results may have been more spectacular, there is little doubt that the most important consequence of developments between 1378 and 1449 was the increased power wielded by secular rulers over their 'national' churches. 'It is not the pope but the king of England who governs the church in his dominions,' Martin V complained. If, as we have seen, kings and princes had already secured considerable influence before 1378, they were subsequently able to exploit the pope's need for allies against the councils to get this influence recognized in the long series of concordats which began with the English concordat of 1418. Everywhere, from Hungary to Spain, developments followed a similar course. In France the Pragmatic Sanction of Bourges was abrogated in 1461; but royal power over the French church remained unimpaired, and what the king had taken at the time of the council of Basel was accorded to him by the pope when Louis XI made a concordat with Pius II in 1472. From 1501 to 1510 the cardinal of Amboise governed the French church in the king's name – much as Wolsey, a little later (and perhaps following the French example), was to govern the English church – and the famous concordat of 1516 left it bound hand and foot to the monarchy. The Italian cities, Venice, Florence, Milan, exercised control every bit as rigorous as that of the kings of France and England. In Spain the reforms of cardinal Ximenes brought the church firmly under the

187

rule of Ferdinand and Isabella; while in Germany, after the concordat of Vienna in 1448, the popes made a series of separate concordats with individual princes, dividing with them the control and profits of their churches.

Three general comments may be made on these developments. First, it was the princes who reaped the benefit of the anti-papal agitation. The reform movement produced no limitation of papal rights, only the transfer of such rights to the prince, or a division of them between prince and pope. In any case, it was the local churches which had to foot the bill. Secondly, though it is often said that the Reformation established lay control over the church, this statement is almost the opposite of the truth. In reality, this was a situation which Luther found in existence and with which he had to cope as best he could. Thirdly, if it is asked why the papacy made the concordats, which were so obviously disadvantageous, the answer is that they assured its theoretical supremacy. If the princes simply usurped papal prerogatives and incorporated them into the constitutional law of their states, they became independent rights. If they were granted by concordat, the pope might theoretically regain them, if in happier circumstances the concordat could be abrogated. At all events, he was recognized as the authority from whom they had to be obtained, with whom the concordat had to be negotiated. The recognition of this fact by the princes, in diplomatic negotiation, assured the pope's supremacy over the council; it buried, so to say, the conciliar theory.

The second result of the conciliar period was a reorganization of papal government. To meet the princes on equal terms, the papacy needed new organs of government, particularly as now the most important decisions affecting the government of the church were negotiated by diplomatic machinery; it also needed new financial resources, particularly when it embarked on an ambitious territorial policy in Italy. Thus, one of the main developments, as, from the time of Martin V, the popes set about putting their house in order, was a reorganization of the papal curia. It was reorganization rather than reform, because it was a question not so much of reforming the old, as of developing new institutions, and bringing the rest into line with the needs of a new age.

In the first place, the chancery and the *camera*, which had been the main vehicles of papal government since the twelfth century, ceased to occupy the central position they had formerly held. The chancery organization remained in existence, but largely for routine business, and many offices became sinecures, sold to the highest bidder. The more responsible work passed instead to new offices, whose connection with the pope was more

93 The new magnificence of the Renaissance papacy; Sixtus IV receiving the Vatican Librarian, Platina

direct and personal. First among these was the 'secretariat' under the pope's 'domestic' or 'secret' secretary – the forerunner of the later 'secretary of state' – which became the main organ of political business and was staffed by first-class men, often drawn from humanist circles (e.g., Poggio Bracciolini). In the same way, the *Signatura* now appeared, with the task of examining all requests for concessions made to the pope. Its emergence as a fixed department with two divisions occurred during the pontificate of Sixtus IV (1471–84), and it was in his pontificate also that the closely related office of the Datary was organized as an independent financial department, controlling the rapidly growing revenues accruing from plenary indulgences and the sale of offices, which by the time of Leo X (1513–21) accounted for no less than one-third of the papal budget. Diplomacy was put on a firm footing by the organization of the papal nuncios, who took the place of the collectors (i.e., tax-gatherers), who had been the local representatives of the papacy since the early fourteenth century. Permanent nuncios – the equivalent of ambassadors – appeared from the time of Sixtus IV, and were directed by and sent in their reports to the secretary of

189

94 Sixtus IV (1471–84), one of the founders of the Renaissance papacy, famous as builder of the Sistine Chapel and for his benefactions to the Vatican Library, which Nicholas V (1447–55) had founded

state. And finally a new type of document, concise, businesslike and written in the new humanistic script – the 'brief' (*breve*) – was introduced in place of the old verbose and formalized papal letters. The 'brief' was the written instrument of the new secretaries. Thus the papacy acquired a 'streamlined' organization, quite on a par with (if not ahead of) that of the rising national states of fifteenth-century Europe; it was in a position to speak to them on terms of equality.

Meeting the European princes on equal terms, negotiating with them as an equal power, the popes themselves became princes. This was perhaps the most conspicuous development of the later fifteenth century. In part, at least, they were helped along this course by the strengthening of Italian nationalism, which was one result of humanism – a movement which looked back to the Roman and Latin past and saw in it an ideal for the Roman and Italian future. From the time of Petrarch in the fourteenth century, Italian humanism was closely related to Italian nationalism. And it is not surprising that the Italian popes of the fifteenth century, far from opposing the new trends of humanism, favoured and promoted them. All the Renaissance popes saw themselves in some degree as representatives of

95 One of the earliest surviving specimens of the papal *breve*; from pope Boniface IX to Francesco Gonzaga of Mantua, 17 October 1390. The new humanistic script had not yet been introduced

the Italian spirit, and as restorers of Italian unity and potential rulers of a united Italy, even though this brought them into conflict with the parallel ambitions of Florence and Milan. But there were more immediate reasons for a restoration of the papacy's position as an Italian territorial power, which had crumbled during the schism. Already under Martin V and Eugenius IV, one of the first tasks had been to restore the papal states. But the reorganization really dates from the pontificates of Paul II (1464–71) and Sixtus IV (1471–84), who profited from the temporary eclipse of Florence after the death of Cosimo de' Medici in 1464, and of Milan after the death of Francesco Sforza in 1466, to build up their power. Finally, under Julius II (1503–13), the papal state was reconstituted in the form it was to retain until the nineteenth century.

It is unnecessary to follow the complicated detail of papal territorial policy, in rivalry with Venice, Florence and Milan, and later steering with difficulty between the French and Spanish invaders. What were important were its results for the papacy; and here two points stand out. First, through its concentration on Italian politics, the papacy lost its universal pretensions and its universal position; it ceased, effectively, to be the head of Christendom, and became instead – and was generally regarded as – one of the Italian powers. Secondly, the popes themselves changed in character. The best were soldiers and warriors, the worst were tyrants, and the morals of more than one – none more so than Alexander VI – were notorious. The

96 Alexander VI (1492–1503), the notorious and profligate Borgia pope; portrait by Pinturicchio

immediate result was that the meagre reforms – or what might more accurately be called the businesslike moderation – of the popes of the first half of the fifteenth century, from Martin V to Nicholas V, gave way again both to fiscalism on a scale unthought of earlier (for example, the wholesale creation of new offices for the sole purpose of selling them), and to nepotism so unashamed (for example, the placing of the pope's illegitimate offspring in the college of cardinals) that it might be thought that Christendom would have revolted in scandal. What is astounding is that it did not; and the fact that it did not is the best evidence that people had, so to say, already 'written off' the papacy; it no longer had any hold over men's minds – not even enough to provoke angry hostility.

And yet the close of the fifteenth and the beginning of the sixteenth centuries were an age of great religious zeal and seriousness. Martin V and Eugenius IV, and Eugenius's successor, Nicholas V (1447–55) – the best pope of the century – made some effort to give this new fervour a lead. Martin V supported Alvarez of Cordova, the apostle of Castile and of Andalusia. Nicholas V sent the great cardinal Nicholas of Cues to lead reform in Germany, and in only two years, from 1451 to 1452, he made remarkable progress – a real indication of what Rome might have achieved, had it only continued to support and guide the strong local movements which were springing up throughout Europe, now that the prospect of general reform had crumbled. But after Nicholas V nothing was done.

98 Coronation of Pius II ▶ (1458–64), the 'humanist pope', a cultivated man of the world, who did not enter the priesthood until he was over forty

97 Nicholas V; one of a series of fifteenth-century portraits of the popes based on the prophecies of Joachim of Fiore. The wolf represents the anti-pope, Felix V, elected at the council of Basel

His successor, Pius II – the famous humanist, Aeneas Silvius – was tepid and half-hearted, too much the cultured scholar to be the religious zealot. After him all was sacrificed to the exigencies of Italian territorial policy.

In effect, the papacy had abdicated its responsibility. Yet reform went on; but the very fact that it went on in particular provinces and dioceses meant growing regionalism and disunity, a tendency for the parts (*membra*) to take care of themselves without reference to the centre or head (*caput*). Among the regular clergy (i.e., the monks) reform was widespread; but it took the form of local congregations. Most famous of all is the Congregation of Windesheim, a congregation of Augustinian Canons reformed by John Busch; hardly less famous were the reformed congregations of Melk and Bursfeld. But it was the same in Italy and France as in Germany – England alone was tepid – and among Cistercians, Carthusians, Carmelites, Dominicans, Franciscans, as well as Augustinians. To revive and reform the secular clergy was a more difficult task; but here also a series of great bishops – such as the Fleming, John Standonck, who became archbishop of Rheims – working through provincial councils, achieved significant results. But the reformers, no longer hoping for effective support from the papacy, looked more and more to kings and secular rulers for backing; and the latter, seeking by the end of the century to establish stricter and more efficient government were more and more inclined to dislike clerical laxity, and to demand austerity. It was characteristic that the great reformers of France and of Spain, the cardinal of Amboise and cardinal Ximenes, both worked hand in glove with the monarchy. It was characteristic; and for the future it was ominous – for if this was the way to get things done, was not the solution, in the end, a state church?

The spirituality of the dying middle ages – inspired largely by the piety of the middle classes – is remarkable in all its aspects, its cults, devotions, charitable practices, its saints and mystics, its edifying literature and prayer and mental turmoil. One should never forget that the great Luther himself came from one of the reformed, observant Augustinian congregations; and his youth, with its ardent asceticism, its torments of conscience, its spiritual strife, is the best evidence of the depth and sincerity of the new devotion. It was a spontaneous revival which occurred in many centres simultaneously, led and inspired by local reformers; but it was not a single great movement, spreading through the whole church, as the Gregorian reform or even the Franciscan movement had been. And so it did not work for the benefit of the church as a whole. Individual churches and congregations were reformed; but the church was not reformed. For this the papacy, without doubt, must be held to account. It abdicated its responsibility, and so it left the way open for Luther, who did not shirk responsibility.

There were powerful religious forces in existence at the close of the fifteenth century, but they needed a leader to canalize them and give them direction. This was Luther's greatest quality. It may be true – as modern historians have sought to show – that there was little, if anything, new in what Luther preached and taught. But he satisfied, as no one else was able to do, the need of the age for a religious leader; hence the huge spontaneous following which flocked to him, long before the princes took a hand in the Reformation. And just as the political aspects of the Reformation were secondary, so also Luther's attack on the papacy was secondary. The movement he led was a religious movement, springing from the deep religious

99 The idyllic spirit of monastic reform: St Gualbertus with the monks of Vallombrosa ▶

feeling of the age; and it was only when, at the council of Trent, the papacy put its house in order, and again took its religious responsibilities seriously, that it was able to compete, and to win back the leadership and esteem which the medieval papacy had forfeited. But Tridentine and post-Tridentine papalism was something new. The medieval papacy ended in bankruptcy, and we may wonder whether, but for Luther, it might not have carried medieval Christendom – or western Christendom – into bankruptcy with it. The gathering of forces, the renewal which he effected, was his great, historical achievement.

Paſſional Chriſti vnd

Er hat funden ym tepel volkauffer/ſchaff/ochſſen vñ tawben vñ wechſler ſitzen/vñ hat gleich eyn geyſſel gemacht võ ſtrickẽ alle ſchaff/ochſſen / taubẽ vñ wechſler auſſem tempell tricben/ das gelt verſchůt/ die zall bredt vmkart vñ zu den die tawben volkaufften geſprochen. Hebt euch hin mit dieſen auß meins vatern hauß/ſolt ir mt ein kauffhauß machẽ.Joh.z.Jr habts vmb ſunſt/darüb gebts vmb ſunſt .Mat. 19. Dein gelt ſey mit dir yn vordamnuß.Act.8

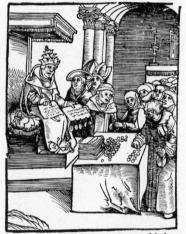

Antichꝛiſt.

Hie ſitzt der Antichꝛiſt ym tẽpell gots vnd erzeygt ſich als got wie Paulus voꝛkundet.z. Teſſal.z.voꝛandert alle gotlich oꝛd/ nung / wie Daniel ſagt / vnnd vntterdruckt die heylig ſchꝛyfft/ voꝛkaufft diſpenſacion/Ablas/Pallia/Biſthum/Lehen/erhebt die ſchetz der erden/löſt auff die che/beſchwoꝛdt die gewiſſen mit ſeynen geſetzen / macht recht / vnnd vmb gelt zureyſt er das/ Erhebt heyligen/benedeyet vñ maledeyet yns vierde geſchlecht vnd gebewt ſein ſtym zuhoꝛen/gleych wie gots ſtym.c. ſic ois. diſt.19.vnd niemants ſall ym eynreden.17.q.4.c. Nemini.

D

100 The burden of the protestant complaint. On the left Christ expels the money-changers from the temple, on the right the pope is seen on his throne, disposing of bishoprics and archbishoprics and selling dispensations and indulgences. As is well known, the sale of plenary indulgences to raise funds for the building of the new St Peter's during the pontificate of Leo X (1513–21) was a major grievance among reformers in Germany

BIBLIOGRAPHICAL NOTES

Owen Chadwick, *The History of the Church. A Select Bibliography* (London:
Historical Association, 1962), contains sections on the papacy. As Professor
Chadwick observes, 'no good and continuous narrative of the medieval
papacy exists in the English language', though there are, of course, many
valuable books on limited aspects or special periods. A good deal of the
more general literature is devotional rather than critical in character, and
most bears the mark of confessional differences. For this reason, it may be
useful, in the following notes, to indicate by appropriate symbols, (C)=
Catholic, (P)=Protestant, (J)=Jewish, the specific approach of at least
some of the leading writers.

Among general histories of the papacy J. Haller (P), *Das Papsttum:
Idee und Wirklichkeit* (paperback ed., 5 vols, Hamburg 1965), is outstanding,
if sometimes highly personal in interpretation. H.K. Mann (C), *The
Lives of the Popes in the Middle Ages* (18 vols, London 1906–32), is con-
scientious and reliable, but mainly useful for reference. It runs to 1304 and
is continued by L. von Pastor (C), *A History of the Popes from the Close of the
Middle Ages,* of which vols 1–6 (London 1891–98) are relevant. C. Mirbt,
Quellen zur Geschichte des Papsttums (4th ed., Tübingen 1924), is the
standard collection of documents; but the selection is now perhaps a
little dated. There are also a number of books dealing with the relations
between the papacy and different countries, e.g. *The English Church and
the Papacy in the Middle Ages,* ed. C.H. Lawrence (London 1965); but
these cannot be listed here.

The history of the papacy naturally looms large in general histories
of the church, of which the best, fullest amd most recent is A. Fliche and
V. Martin (C), *Histoire de l'église* (vols 1–15, Paris 1934–64). P. Hughes (C),
A History of the Church (3 vols, London 1934–37), is a shorter account in
English, which describes itself as 'an introductory study'. I have also found
A. Dufourcq (C), *L'Avenir du Christianisme,* vols 3–7 (7th ed., Paris
1930–34), stimulating, if rather uneven; the rather surprising title hides
a straightfoward historical approach. Essential also are histories of the
canon law. Most recent, and of high quality, is H.E. Feine (P), *Kirchliche
Rechtsgeschichte,* vol. 1: *Die katholische Kirche* (3rd ed., Weimar 1955),

but the classic work of P. Hinschius (P), *Das Kirchenrecht der Katholiken und Protestanten in Deutschland* (6 vols, Berlin 1869–97), covers more ground and is still indispensable. J. B. Sägmüller (C), *Lehrbuch des katholischen Kirchenrechts* (4th ed., Freiburg i. B. 1925–34), is a useful compendium, and there is an excellent short, but little known, volume by A. M. Koeniger (C), *Grundriss einer Geschichte des katholischen Kirchenrechtes* (Cologne 1919). Little, so far, has appeared of G. le Bras (C), *Histoire du droit et des institutions de l'église en occident* (Paris 1956–); but vol. 7 (1140–1378) gives an up-to-date account of legal developments beginning with Gratian.

A great deal of learning and speculation have latterly been expended, with rather meagre results, on the theoretical foundations of papal government. There is still no substitute for R. W. and A. J. Carlyle (P), *A History of Mediaeval Political Theory in the West* (6 vols, Edinburgh 1903–36), where most of the essential material is summarized and discussed; but there is good sense in the short book by R. Hull (C), *Medieval Theories of the Papacy* (London 1934). For more recent views, it is perhaps sufficient to refer to the volume *Sacerdozio e Regno da Gregorio VII a Bonifacio VIII*, ed. F. Kempf (C), (Rome 1954), with valuable papers by A. M. Stickler (C) and M. Maccarrone (C); but one of the best short statements can be found in Father Kempf's own survey, 'Die päpstliche Gewalt in der mittelalterlichen Welt', *Miscellanea Historiae Pontificiae*, vol. XXI (Rome 1959), which takes issue with W. Ullmann, *The Growth of Papal Government in the Middle Ages* (2nd ed., London 1962), a learned but idiosyncratic book, which should be treated with caution. Another more general book, also largely concerned with theory, is T. G. Jalland (P), *The Church and the Papacy* (London 1944).

THE PAPACY IN THE ROMAN EMPIRE This is not the place to list or discuss the numerous general histories of the early church. The best, in my view, is still L. Duchesne (C), *Early History of the Christian Church* (3 vols, London 1909–24), which, though superseded in parts, remains a masterly survey. It may be supplemented by H. Lietzmann (P), *A History of the Early Church* (4 vols, 2nd ed., London 1949–51), probably the best of the more recent accounts. Both give considerable attention to the church of Rome. On the papacy itself, Haller's first volume, though relatively short, is indispensable. Much fuller is E. Caspar (J), *Geschichte des Papsttums* (2 vols, Tübingen 1930–33). This is usually regarded as the standard work from the beginnings to 752, but it does not seem to me quite to live up to its high reputation. There is also an impressive survey, extending from 480 to 882, by H. von Schubert (P),

Geschichte der christlichen Kirche im Frühmittelalter (Tübingen 1921), and the political background is surveyed by F. Lot, *La fin du monde antique et le début du moyen âge* (Paris 1927). Reference may also be made to the biographies of *St. Leo the Great* (London 1941) by T.G. Jalland (P), and of *Gregory the Great* (2 vols, Oxford 1905) by F.H. Dudden (P).

The more doctrinal aspects of the rise of the papacy are dealt with, shortly and clearly, by B.J. Kidd (P), *The Roman Primacy to A.D. 461* (London 1936). M.M. Winter (C), *Saint Peter and the Popes* (London 1960), covers the same ground from a different angle, and H. Burn-Murdoch, *The Development of the Papacy* (London 1954), has attempted an objective presentation of both sides of the argument. The basic texts are assembled, in translation, by E. Giles (P), *Documents illustrating Papal Authority, A.D. 96–454* (London 1952), and there is a similar, but fuller, compilation, with useful annotations, by J.T. Shotwell and L.R. Loomis (P), *The See of Peter* (New York 1927).

H. von Schubert's volume remains the best general account, but, on a smaller scale, L. Duchesne (C), *Les premiers temps de l'état pontifical* (3rd ed., Paris 1911; English translation, 1908), is brief, intelligent and lucid, and unsurpassed within its compass. The history of the temporal power of the papacy was continued, though in a narrower framework, by D. Waley, *The Papal State in the Thirteenth Century* (London 1961), and the main documentary sources were printed by J. Haller (P), *Quellen zur Geschichte der Entstehung des Kirchenstaates* (2nd ed., Leipzig 1914). E. Caspar, *Das Papsttum unter fränkischer Herrschaft* (Darmstadt 1956), was intended as a continuation of his history of the papacy and originally appeared in the *Zeitschrift für Kirchengeschichte,* vol. LIV (1935), before being reprinted in book form. Among the special studies of the early relations between the Carolingians and the papacy, it is sufficient to mention the two older works of E. Caspar, *Pippin und die römische Kirche* (Berlin 1914), and J. Haller, 'Die Karolinger und das Papsttum', *Historische Zeitschrift,* vol. CVIII (1912). With the exception of L. Levillain, 'L'avènement de la dynastie carolingienne et les origines de l'état pontifical', *Bibliothèque de l'école des chartes,* vol. XCIV (1933), the numerous subsequent investigations, in spite of a great expenditure of learning, have done little to bring about further elucidation of the problems.

The view that contact with the Germanic peoples, particularly the Anglo-Saxons, resulted in a revolutionary transformation of the position of the bishop of Rome, was argued with great verve by Haller, both in his history of the papacy and earlier. It was perhaps stated in an exaggerated way, and was hotly contested; but it seems to me to contain an essential truth. The standard account of the Anglo-Saxon missions and their impact is W. Levison (J), *England and the Continent in the Eighth Century* (Oxford 1946), but it should be supplemented by T. Zwölfer, *Sankt Peter Apostelfürst und Himmelspförtner* (Stuttgart 1929), an illuminating study of the spread of the cult of St Peter, and by the more recent and wider ranging book of T. Schieffer, *Winfrid-Bonifatius und die christliche Grundlegung Europas* (Freiburg i. B. 1954).

Among general books on the later Carolingian period it is sufficient to mention H. Fichtenau (C), *The Carolingian Empire* (Oxford 1957), and L. Halphen (J), *Charlemagne et l'empire carolingien* (Paris 1947), the latter particularly good for ninth-century developments. The best critical account of the events of 800 is still K. Heldmann, *Das Kaisertum Karls des Grossen* (Weimar 1928). J.M. Wallace-Hadrill's short and illuminating study of the king's position in relation to the church, in *Trends in Medieval Political Thought,* ed. B. Smalley (Oxford 1965), is well worth reading, and H.X. Arquillière, *L'augustinisme politique* (Paris 1934), is useful for Nicholas I, on whom there is no good modern book.

THE AGE OF REFORM Much has been written on the reform movement both before and at the time of Gregory VII. Only a short selection can be listed here. The standard account, now a little dated, is A. Fliche (C), *La réforme grégorienne* (3 vols, Louvain 1924–37), and should be compared with G. Tellenbach (P), *Church, State and Christian Society at the Time of the Investiture Contest* (Oxford 1940). Later work is best followed in the volumes of *Studi Gregoriani,* ed. G.B. Borino, of which the first volume appeared in Rome in 1947. There is also a good conspectus of the whole reform movement in U. Berlière (C), *L'ordre monastique des origines au XIIe siècle* (3rd ed., Maredsous 1924), and a stimulating essay by Norman F. Cantor, 'The Crisis of Western Monasticism, 1050–1130', *American Historical Review,* LXVI (1960).

The best short characterization of Gregory VII is still that of E. Caspar (J), 'Gregor VII. in seinen Briefen', *Historische Zeitschrift,* CXXX (1924). The resistance of the great metropolitan churches to Gregory is examined, in one key instance, by O. Meyer (P), 'Reims und Rom unter Gregor VII.', *Zeitschrift der Savigny-Stiftung für Rechtsgeschichte, kanon. Abt.,* LIX (1939), and the question of Milan by J.P. Whitney (P), *Hildebrandine Essays* (Cambridge 1932). The part played by the question of investitures, usually exaggerated, is well set out by Z. N. Brooke (P), 'Lay Investiture and its relation to the Conflict of Empire and Papacy', *Proceedings of the British Academy*, vol. xxv (1939). Some of the main texts were printed by W. Fritz, *Quellen zum Wormser Konkordat* (Berlin 1955).

There is a good account of developments from Gregory VII to 1130 by F. J. Schmale, 'Papsttum und Kurie zwischen Gregor VII. und Innocenz II.', *Historische Zeitschrift*, CXCIII (1961). For the pontificates of Eugenius III (1145–53) and Hadrian IV (1154–59) no really adequate studies are available. For Alexander III there is M. Pacaut (C), *Alexandre III. Étude* *sur la conception du pouvoir pontifical dans sa pensée et dans son œuvre* (Paris 1956), but this, though valuable so far as it goes, is largely concerned with theory, and H. Reuter (P), *Geschichte Alexanders III. und der Kirche seiner Zeit* (Leipzig 1860), is out-dated. The history of the papacy between Alexander III and Innocent III is admirably treated by K. Wenck (P), 'Die römischen Päpste zwischen Alexander III. und Innocenz III.', in *Papsttum und Kaisertum*, ed. A. Brackmann (Munich 1926). For Innocent III the standard work is still A. Luchaire, *Innocent III* (6 vols, Paris 1905–08); there is also a short life by L. E. Binns (P), *Innocent III* (London 1931), and a judicious chapter by E. F. Jacob (P), in the *Cambridge Medieval History*, vol. VI, ch. 1. Among the numerous studies of Innocent III's views of the pope's position and of the relations of church and state, one of the better and more recent is F. Kempf (C), *Papsttum und Kaisertum bei Innocenz III* (Rome 1954).

The chapters by E. W. Watson (P), 'The Development of Ecclesiastical Organisation' (vol. 6, ch. 16), and H. D. Hazeltine (P), 'Roman and Canon Law in the Middle Ages' (vol. 5, ch. 21), in the *Cambridge Medieval History* are useful as a starting-point. For the development of canon law, the sub- ject of much work in recent years, the basic work is P. Fournier and G. le Bras (C), *Histoire des collections canoniques en occident* (2 vols, Paris 1931–32), and Fournier summarized his results in a capital article of lasting importance, 'Un tournant de l'histoire du droit', *Nouvelle revue historique de droit,* vol. XLI (1917). There is a good and full analysis of the work of Gratian in R. Sohm (P), *Das altkatholische Kirchenrecht und das Dekret Gratians* (Leipzig 1918). This was attacked by Stutz, because Sohm empha-sized the theological connotations of Gratian's work and refused him the title of 'father of canon law', and has consequently received less than due recognition; it is nevertheless extremely perceptive. For the development of canon law after Gratian the basic work is S. Kuttner (C), *Repertorium der Kanonistik, 1140–1234* (Vatican City 1937). For the period after 1234, in spite of much work in detail, there is still nothing to take the place of J. F. von Schulte (C), *Geschichte der Quellen und Literatur des canonischen Rechts* (3 vols, Stuttgart 1875–80).

There has been much important work in recent years on the development of the institutions of the papal monarchy after Leo IX, but so far no synthesis. The best starting-point is K. Jordan (P), *Die Entstehung der römischen Kurie* (Darmstadt 1962), which originally appeared in the *Zeitschrift der Savigny-Stiftung für Rechtsgeschichte*, vol. LIX (1939), and another article by the same author, 'Die päpstliche Verwaltung im Zeitalter Gregors VII', *Studi Gregoriani*, vol. I (1947), which may be supplemented by J. Sydow, 'Untersuchungen zur kurialen Verwaltungsgeschichte im Zeitalter des Reformpapsttums', *Deutsches Archiv für Erforschung des Mittelalters*, vol. XI (1954). For the cardinals, H. W. Klewitz (P), *Reformpapsttum und Kardinalkolleg* (Darmstadt 1957), including the article, 'Die Entstehung des Kardinalkollegiums', *Zeitschrift der Savigny-Stiftung . . .*, vol. LVI (1936), is basic. Important also is S. Kuttner (C), 'Cardinalis: The History of a Canonical Concept', *Traditio*, vol. III (1945), and for later developments J. B. Sägmüller (C), *Die Thätigkeit und Stellung der Cardinäle bis Papst Bonifaz VIII* (Freiburg i. B. 1896), though old, is still useful.

The financial organization is exhaustively dealt with by W. E. Lunt (P), *Papal Revenues in the Middle Ages* (2 vols, New York 1934), the penitentiary by E. Göller (C), *Die päpstliche Pönitentiarie* (Rome 1907), the chapel and chaplains by R. Elze, 'Die päpstliche Kapelle im 12. und 13. Jahrhundert', *Zeitschrift der Savigny-Stiftung . . .*, vol. LXVII (1950), and the law-courts by F. E. Schneider (C), *Die römische Rota* (Paderborn 1914). B. Rusch, *Die Behörden und Hofbeamten der päpstlichen Kurie des 13. Jahrhunderts* (Königsberg 1936), is a useful compilation. The position in regard to the papal chancery (on the word, which was not used until after 1180, cf. H. W. Klewitz, 'Cancellaria', *Deutsches Archiv*, vol. I, 1937) is less satisfactory. H. Bresslau, *Handbuch der Urkundenlehre*, vol. I (2nd ed., Leipzig 1912), still contains the best general account, but is no longer up to date; the same applies to R. L. Poole, *Lectures on the History of the Papal Chancery* (Cambridge 1915), which, however, usefully summarizes in English the arguments of the famous article by P. F. Kehr (P), 'Scrinium und Palatium', *Mitteilungen des Instituts für österreichische Geschichtsforschung*, Erg. Bd. VI (1901), in which the basic changes leading to the rise of the chancery are traced. The important developments under Innocent III, which in effect amounted to the emergence of the chancery as a separate office of state, are best followed in the various articles of R. von Heckel (C), in *Miscellanea Francesco Ehrle,* vol. II (Rome 1924), *Festschrift für A. Brackmann* (Weimar 1931), *Hist. Jahrbuch,* vol. LVII (1937), etc. For thirteenth-century developments, there is a recent and learned study by P. Herde, *Beiträge zum päpstlichen Kanzlei- und Urkundenwesen im 13. Jahrhundert* (Kallmünz 1961).

Most aspects of the extension of papal control over the church have been examined. F. W. Maitland (P), *Roman Canon Law in the Church of England* (London 1898), is good on the pope as 'universal ordinary'. Z. N. Brooke (P), *The English Church and the Papacy* (Cambridge 1931), and C. R. Cheney (P), *From Becket to Langton* (Manchester 1956), discuss the process by which the new law of the decretals was gradually applied and built up. G. Barraclough, 'The Making of a Bishop in the Middle Ages', *Catholic Historical Review,* vol. XIX (1933), and *Papal Provisions* (Oxford 1935), traces the growth of papal control over episcopal elections and appointments to minor benefices respectively. E. W. Kemp (P), *Canonization and Authority in the Western Church* (Oxford 1948), shows how the pope established an exclusive right to sanction the veneration of saints, and A. J. Macdonald (P), *Authority and Reason in the Early Middle Ages* (Oxford 1933), how the papacy became 'the adjudicator of doctrine'. A. Hauck (P), 'Die Rezeption und Umbildung der allgemeinen Synode im Mittelalter', *Hist. Vierteljahrsschrift,* vol. X (1907), traces the stages by which the general councils of the church were brought under papal control.

The best introduction, in spite of its age, is J. Haller (P), *Papsttum und Kirchenreform* (Berlin 1903). There are also two general histories, both beginning in the thirteenth century and extending to the end of the middle ages, fairly adequate in matter, but not quite up to the level of recent study: they are L. E. Binns (P), *The Decline and Fall of the Medieval Papacy* (London 1934), and A. C. Flick (P), *The Decline of the Medieval Church* (2 vols, London 1930). A. L. Smith (P), *Church and State in the Middle Ages* (Oxford 1933), is an attempt to pin-point the dilemmas confronting the papacy around the middle of the thirteenth century; although all its conclusions would no longer be accepted, it makes some important points. I also derived much profit from K. Schleyer, *Anfänge des Gallikanismus im 13. Jahrhundert* (Berlin 1937), an able account of the resistance of the French prelates to papal centralization. There is a lively biography of

Boniface VIII (London 1933) by T.S.R. Boase (P), and a standard book on the controversies of his pontificate is J. Rivière (C), *Le problème de l'église et de l'état au temps de Philippe le Bel* (Louvain 1926); E. Renan, *Études sur la politique religieuse du règne de Philippe le Bel* (Paris 1899), is also still well worth reading, particularly for Clement V.

The standard account for the fourteenth century, perhaps rather too favourable, is G. Mollat (C), *The Popes at Avignon* (Edinburgh 1963); but there is also a good short history by Y. Renouard, *La papauté à Avignon* (Paris 1954), and an able essay by B. Smalley (C), in *Europe in the Late Middle Ages,* ed. J.R. Hale, J.R.L. Highfield and B. Smalley (London 1965). A short book by E. Kraack, *Rom oder Avignon* (Marburg 1929), is also illuminating, as well as the articles by F. Bock (P), 'Kaisertum, Kurie und Nationalstaat im Beginn des 14. Jahrhunderts', *Römische Quartalschrift*, vol. XLIV (1936).

N. Valois, *La France et le grand schisme* (4 vols, Paris 1896–1902), and *Le pape et le concile, 1418–50* (2 vols, Paris 1909), are still the basic narrative for the period after 1378. M. Creighton (P), *A History of the Papacy from the Great Schism to the Sack of Rome* (2nd ed., London 1903–05), also retain its value. Reference may also be made to M. Seidlmayer (C), *Die Anfänge des grossen abendländischen Schismas* (Stuttgart 1940), and W. Ullmann (C), *The Origins of the Great Schism* (London 1948), and B. Tierney (C), *Foundations of the Conciliar Theory* (Cambridge 1955), is excellent for the antecedents. E.F. Jacob (P), *Essays in the Conciliar Epoch* (2nd ed., Manchester 1953), is good, and largely supersedes J.N. Figgis (P), *From Gerson to Grotius* (2nd ed., Cambridge 1916). Among more specialized writing, there is an account of the 'subtraction of obedience' by G. Barraclough in *Revue d'histoire ecclésiastique,* vol. XXX (1934), and most of the leading personalities in the conciliar movement have been the subject of monographs, e.g. J.P. MacGowen (C), *Pierre d'Ailly* (Washington, D.C. 1936), J.B. Morrall, *Gerson and the Great Schism* (Manchester 1960), P.E. Sigmund, *Nicolas of Cusa* (Cambridge, Mass. 1963).

THE RENAISSANCE PAPACY The general works of Pastor, Creighton, Dufourcq (vol. 7), Elliott Binns and Flick, cited above, are all relevant, and J. Guiraud (C), *L'église romaine et les origines de la renaissance* (5th ed., Paris 1921), is still a useful short introduction; but the outstanding work for the whole fifteenth century is now the first (introductory) book of H. Jedin (C), *A History of the Council of Trent,* vol. I (London 1957). For the reorganization of the Roman curia, W. von Hofmann (P), *Forschungen zur Geschichte der kurialen Behörden vom*

Schisma bis zur Reformation (2 vols, Rome 1914), remains essential. On the territorial policy of the fifteenth-century popes reference may be made to P. Partner, *The Papal State under Martin V* (London 1958), and J. Guiraud, *L'état pontifical après le grand schisme* (Paris 1896). G. von Below (P), *Die Ursachen der Reformation* (Munich 1917), and J. Haller (P), *Die Ursachen der Reformation* (Tübingen 1917), fill in the background; but perhaps the best general survey of the pre-Reformation church is now to be found in G. G. Coulton (P), *Five Centuries of Religion*, vol. IV (Cambridge 1950).

LIST OF ILLUSTRATIONS

25 The four parts of the empire: Slavinia, Germania, Gallia and Roma; miniature from Gospel book of Otto III, 997–1000. Staatsbibliothek, Munich. Photo: Max Hirmer

26 Otto III; miniature from Gospel book of Otto III, 997–1000. Staatsbibliothek, Munich. Photo: Max Hirmer

27 Capital from the abbey of Cluny, Saône-et-Loire, showing the first tone of plainsong, c. 1095. Musée Ochier, Cluny. Photo: Veronèse

28 Cluny; south-western transept and crossing tower, 1088–1135. Photo: Veronèse

29 Map of monastic reform movement in the tenth and eleventh centuries; drawn by S. Schotten

30 Dedication of third abbey church of Cluny; miniature from the *Book of Offices and Chronicon Cluniacense* of St-Martin-des-Champs, Paris, late twelfth century. Bibliothèque Nationale, Paris

31 Liturgical scene 'Incensi huius sacrificium'; from exultet roll, Monte Cassino, eleventh century. Vatican Library

32 Pope Leo IX and abbot Warinus of St Arnulf; miniature from manuscript done in Metz, second half of eleventh century. Burgbibliothek, Bern

33 Emperor Henry III between two bishops; from the *Evangelium of Henry III, c.* 1040. Staatsbibliothek, Bremen

34 Emperor Henry IV; miniature from the *Weltchronik* of Ekkehard of Aura, 1113–14. Corpus Christi College, Cambridge

35 Henry IV expels Gregory VII; miniature from the *Weltchronik* of Otto of Freising, 1170. Universitätsbibliothek, Jena

36 The *Dictatus Papae,* entered in the register of pope Gregory VII under the year 1075. Vatican Archives

37 Armed knights in the period of the First Crusade; miniature from the Commentary on the Apocalypse by the monk Beatus, executed in the monastery of San Domingo de Silos, Spain, c. 1109. British Museum

38 First page of the *Decretum* of Gratian; Bolognese, twelfth century. Biblioteca Marciana, Venice

39 Pope Paschal II with scribe; marginal drawing from the *Chronicon Vulturnense*, 1124–30. Vatican Library

40 Pope Gelasius II; miniature from the *Cronaca di S. Sofia,* mid-twelfth century. Vatican Library

41 Popes and anti-popes; pen and ink drawings of lost frescoes in the chamber of secret councils in the old Lateran palace, second half of sixteenth century. Vatican Library

42 Crowning of Lothar III by pope Innocent II; pen and ink drawings of lost frescoes in the chamber of secret councils in the old Lateran palace, second half of sixteenth century. Vatican Library

43 St Bernard of Clairvaux; detail of the altarpiece of St Bernard, by the Master of Palma. Palma de Mallorca

44 Bull of Eugenius III (obverse); facsimile. British Museum. Photo: Freeman

45 Frederick Barbarossa; gilded reliquary bearing the emperor's features, end of twelfth century. Stift Kappenberg, Germany

46 A concilium; drawing from a *collectio canonum,* eleventh century. Vatican Library

47 Pope Celestine III crowning Henry VI in Rome; miniature from the Chronicle of Petrus de Ebulo, end of twelfth century. Burgbibliothek, Bern

48 Pope Innocent III; fresco in the lower church of Sacro Speco, Subiaco, thirteenth century. Photo: Mansell/Alinari

49, 50 The Fourth Crusade: pavement mosaics of S. Giovanni Evangelista, Ravenna. Photo: Mansell/Anderson

51 St Peter in pontifical robes; statue in St Peter's, Rome, fourteenth century. Photo: Mansell/Anderson

52 'Decretals' of Gregory IX; illumination from the *Smithfield Decretals*, English, early fourteenth century. British Museum

53 Philip the Fair; statue in the abbey of St-Denis. Photo: Giraudon

54 Pope Boniface VIII; statue attributed to Arnolfo di Cambio in the Cathedral Museum, Florence. Photo: Mansell/Alinari

55 The pope in council; miniature from a manuscript of the *Decretum Gratiani*, Spanish, end of the fourteenth century. British Museum

56 Boniface VIII with the college of cardinals; miniature from a manuscript of the *Liber Sextus* of Boniface, Bolognese, fourteenth century. British Museum

57 Fourth Lateran Council (1215); marginal drawing by Matthew Paris from *Cronica Maiora*. Corpus Christi College, Cambridge

58 St Dominic; portrait attributed to Guido da Siena, thirteenth century. Bequest of Hervey E. Wetzel, 1911, by courtesy of the Fogg Art Museum, Harvard University

59 St Francis of Assisi; detail of *The Madonna of St Francis*, fresco by Cimabue, late thirteenth century. Lower church of S. Francesco, Assisi. Photo: Marzari

60 The Holy Trinity; a page from Joachim of Fiore's *I tre regni e la Trinità*, end of thirteenth century. Vatican Library

61 Franciscan and Dominican friars; marginal illustration from *De pauperie salvatoris* by Richard Fitzralph, archbishop of Armagh, mid-fourteenth century. Corpus Christi College, Cambridge

62 *The Dream of Innocent III;* fresco by Giotto in upper church of S. Francesco, Assisi, end thirteenth century. Photo: Scala

63, 64 Illustrations to Dante's *Divine Comedy*, Sienese, first half of fifteenth century. British Museum

65 Clement V(?); detail of Andrea di Firenze's fresco *Triumph of the Church*, S. Maria Novella, Florence, 1366–68. Photo: Mansell/Alinari

66 Election of pope John XXII; miniature from the *Cronaca Villani*, second half of fourteenth century. Vatican Library

67 Pope judging heretics; Bolognese, end of fourteenth century. Staatliche Museen der Stiftung Preussischer Kulturbesitz, Berlin

68 Palace of the Popes, Avignon; pen and wash drawing, seventeenth century. Musée Calvet, Avignon

69 Benedict XII; statue by Paolo de Siena, 1341. Vatican Grottoes. Photo: Mansell/Anderson

70 Coronation of pope Clement VI; miniature from the *Cronaca Villani,* second half of fourteenth century. Vatican Library

71 Pope Clement VI; caricature, from manuscript illustrating the prophecies of Joachim of Fiore about the popes, north Italian, fifteenth century. Österreichische Nationalbibliothek, Vienna

72 St Catherine of Siena; fresco by Francesco Vanni in the church of S. Domenico, Siena, 1596. Photo: Mansell/Alinari

73 *Crucifixion;* painting by Giunta Pisano, thirteenth century. Church of S. Matteo, Pisa. Photo: Scala

74 Burial of plague-victims; miniature from the *Annales* of Gilles le Muisit, Flemish, 1352. Bibliothèque Royale de Belgique, Brussels

75 Papal Loggia of the Bishop's Palace, Viterbo; thirteenth century. Photo: Mansell/Anderson

76 Pope Urban V returning to Rome; miniature, fourteenth century. Musée Calvet, Avignon

77 Sarcophagus of pope Urban VI; 1389. Vatican Grottoes. Photo: Mansell/Alinari

78 Pope Boniface IX; statue in the basilica of S. Paolo fuori le mura, fourteenth century. Photo: Mansell/Alinari

79 Christ washing the disciples' feet; miniature from a Hussite manuscript, second half of the fifteenth century. Knihovna Narodniho Muzea, Prague

80 A pope with monks at his feet; miniature from a Hussite manuscript, second half of the fifteenth century. Knihovna Narodniho Muzea, Prague

81 Monks and nuns; anti-clerical satire from the Hussite *Mirror of Christendom,* written in Bohemia, second half of fifteenth century. Universitätsbibliothek, Göttingen

82 Comment on religion and pleasure; miniature from a Hussite manuscript, second half of the fifteenth century. Knihovna Narodniho Muzea, Prague

83 Effigy of Charles V; abbey of St-Denis, Paris, fourteenth century. Photo: Giraudon

84 Pope John XXIII; monument by Donatello in the Baptistery, Florence, 1425–27. Photo: Mansell/Alinari

85 John Hus at the stake; miniature from Ulrich von Reichental's *Chronicle of the Council of Constance,* Bohemian, first half of fifteenth century. Facsimile copy in British Museum

86 John Žižka leading the Hussite army; miniature from the Hussite *Mirror of Christendom,* Bohemian, second half of fifteenth century. Universitätsbibliothek, Göttingen

87 Constance; from *Civitate Orbis Terrarum,* end of sixteenth century. British Museum. Photo: Freeman

88 Pope Martin V; bronze relief for his grave, by Donatello and Michelozzo, basilica of St John in Lateran, 1433. Photo: Mansell/Alinari

89 Pope Eugenius IV crowning Sigismund emperor; bronze relief from the doors of St Peter's by Filarete, 1435–45. Photo: Mansell/Anderson

90 Seal of the council of Basel. Kunsthistorisches Museum, Vienna

91 Coronation of Frederick III; painting by a Flemish master of the second half of the fifteenth century. Germanisches Nationalmuseum, Nuremberg

92 St Peter's; sixteenth-century painting. Vatican Library. Photo: Mansell/Alinari

93 Platina received as Vatican Librarian by Sixtus IV, fresco by Melozzo da Forlì, 1477. Vatican Galleries, Photo: Archivio Fotografico Gallerìe e Musei Vaticani

94 Pope Sixtus IV; effigy from the monument by Antonio del Pollaiuolo, 1490–93. Vatican Grottoes. Photo: Mansell/Alinari

95 The first *breve,* 17 October 1390. By courtesy of the Archivo di Stato, Mantua

96 Pope Alexander VI; detail from the frescoes in the Borgia apartments in the Vatican by Pinturicchio, 1492–95. Photo: Mansell/Alinari

97 Nicholas V; caricature from manuscript illustrating the prophecies of Joachim of Fiore about the popes, north Italian, fifteenth century. Österreichische Nationalbibliothek, Vienna

98 Coronation of Pius II; painting by the school of Giovanni di Paolo, fifteenth century. Archivio di Stato, Siena. Photo: Mansell/Anderson

99 St Gualbertus with the monks of Vallombrosa; anonymous drawing, *c.* 1400. Kupferstichkabinett, Berlin

100 Anti-papal woodcuts by Lucas Cranach, 1521. British Museum. Photo: Freeman

INDEX

Page numbers in italics refer to illustrations

213